Service-Learning

From Classroom to Community to Career

MARIE WATKINS, PH.D.

LINDA BRAUN

jist
Life

Service-Learning

From Classroom to Community to Career

© 2005 by Marie Watkins and Linda Braun

Published by JIST Life, an imprint of JIST Publishing, Inc.
8902 Otis Avenue
Indianapolis, IN 46216-1033
Phone: 1-800-648-JIST   Fax: 1-800-JIST-FAX
E-mail: info@jist.com   Web site: www.jist.com

Visit our Web site at **www.jist.com** for more information on JIST, free job search tips, book excerpts, and ordering instructions on our many products! For free information on 14,000 job titles, visit **www.careeroink.com.**

A note to instructors: An instructor's manual (ISBN 1-55864-151-3) is available for this book. It provides outlines, activities for assessment, and background information for each chapter of the workbook.

Quantity discounts are available for JIST books. Please call our Sales Department at 1-800-648-JIST for a free catalog and more information.

Acquisitions Editor: Barb Terry
Development Editor: Jennifer Eberhardt
Production Editor: Heather Stith
Copy Editor: Chuck Hutchinson
Interior Designer: Aleata Howard
Illustrator: Katherine Knutson
Page Layout: Carolyn J. Newland
Proofreaders: Linda Seifert, Jeanne Clark
Indexer: Kelly D. Henthorne

Printed in Canada

10 09 08 07 06 05   9 8 7 6 5 4 3 2 1

ISBN 1-55864-150-5

About This Book

This book is designed to be a student-friendly guidebook to prepare and inform you about the how-tos of service-learning, with tried-and-true strategies that will help you to be successful as you learn academic material while performing an off-campus service. Throughout this guidebook, you will be introduced to a variety of topics that will help you understand how service can help you learn as a person, student, and prospective career professional. Whether your field of study is math, music, English, computer technology, or some other area of interest; and whether your career goal is business, education, human services, health sciences, or any other area, service-learning can help you to achieve your goals.

Acknowledgements

Dr. Watkins and Ms. Braun acknowledge that this book is the result of the support of many family members, friends, and colleagues at Nazareth College:

Dr. Watkins's parents taught her to be of service to others in a kind and humble manner, and their caring spirits continue to guide her. She also appreciates the cooked meals and hugs provided by her husband, Bob McCarthy. And from her best buddy, Bella, Dr. Watkins has learned how a pet can teach acts of unconditional love and service. Ms. Braun would like to thank her parents for raising her to understand the importance of a good work ethic, a sound education, and giving back to the community. Ms. Braun would also like thank her dear friends Glenn and Eileen Call for their support and encouragement while the book was "under construction."

We thank the many service-learning champions at Nazareth College in Rochester, New York: Sister Kathy Weider, SSJ, founding director of the Center for Service-Learning; Dr. Robert Miller, former president; Dr. Dennis Silva, Vice President for Academic Affairs; Professor Al Cabral, Chairperson of Nazareth's Campus Compact Committee; Mary Ann Chiella, Coordinator of Graduate Students; and Alex Shukoff, Campus Photographer. This book would not have been possible without the cooperation of faculty and students. We thank Drs. Leeanne Charlesworth, Mary Ellen Potts, Phyllis Ladrigan, and Edward Wiltse and Professor Annemarie House for their contribution of student journals. We appreciate the service ideas put into practice by Drs. Beverly Brown, Otieno Kisiari, Harry Murray, Susan Nowak, Bryan Hunter, and Joseph Daboll-Lavoie, and Professor Roy Stein. And most of all, we thank our Nazareth College students for their service-learning energy and commitment, especially Megan Hughes, Joy Messenger, Yolanda Mitnaul, and Shawn Ryan.

Finally, we thank the editors at JIST Publishing, Inc., for their collegial partnership with us. JIST's collaborative approach is truly an example of the best practices of service-learning!

Contents

Introduction

It's the first day of class. Excited and nervous, you and your classmates look over the course objectives. You recognize the familiar class requirements—reading certain books, taking regularly scheduled tests—and then, what's this? You learn that you must participate in a service-learning project that relates to the course objectives. But what is service-learning, and how will it help you to achieve course objectives and personal goals?

Service-Learning Is...

One common misconception is that service-learning is the same as volunteering, but there are distinct differences. For example, you'll learn course materials in a service-learning project by connecting a needed community service to your course objectives. (You'll learn more about this connection in Chapter 2.)

Service-learning encompasses many different types of activities. Some examples of service-learning include the following:

- Creating or participating in a recycling program for your school or community that helps you to understand your environmental education course

- Mentoring younger students in academic studies or through peer programs to increase your knowledge of child development

- Lobbying state officials to pass laws of local concern as an assignment in your political science class

- Sponsoring a food drive to learn the connection between social action and the fundamentals of economics in an economics class

And with each of these examples in which "in-class" subject learning is connected with "outside of class" service, there is an ongoing process of reflection: What did I learn? How does this information connect? Why is it important? These are just a few examples of service-learning. Throughout this book, you will find more ideas that you can explore and put into practice.

Why We Wrote This Book

This guidebook was prompted by the experiences of students who have participated in service-learning courses and by our own experiences as college students, career professionals, and educators. Students tell us that their service-learning projects are much more meaningful when the students are prepared and guided to achieve their service-learning course objectives in a well-planned way, with the teacher or professor and the agency staff all on the same page. We understand the students' anxiety, the faculty's good intentions, and the community-based partners' sense of being overwhelmed.

This guidebook reflects the common ideas that emerged from a review of more than 200 student reflection papers written by undergraduate students from a variety of academic disciplines who attended Nazareth College, an upstate New York liberal arts college. Students shared their insights in a variety of areas:

- Perceptions of the ingredients of a meaningful service-learning experience

- Fears and anxieties about the service-learning experience

- Situations for which students wished they had been forewarned or better prepared

- Tremendous personal and professional growth resulting from the service-learning experience

Many of the lessons learned by our students were similar to the ones that had enhanced and affected our own college educations, and we wanted to share those lessons.

How to Use This Book

For you to be better prepared to make a valuable contribution to the community and complete your course requirements through service-learning, you need to have direction, information, and opportunities for reflection to help you to accomplish these specific goals:

- Plan for a successful experience.

- Assess what you've learned.

- Reflect on how you've grown.

- Celebrate what you've contributed to the community.

- Connect your service-learning experience to your professional development goals.

The chapters of this book are designed to help you achieve each of these goals.

Chapter 1, "Exploring the Idea of Service-Learning," begins where you are right now—with a general idea of what service-learning is all about and a lot of questions about exactly how service-learning fits into your specific academic program. We briefly review some of the comments of college students who enjoyed their service-learning experiences and felt that they learned something important in a unique way.

Chapter 2, "Understanding the Fundamentals of Service-Learning," provides you with a foundation for thinking about the educational process—different ways of learning and different ways of teaching. Service-learning is explored as a teaching strategy to help students learn.

Chapter 3, "Learning about Yourself through Service," gives you an opportunity to reflect about your educational goals, your goals for your professional development, and the way service-learning can help you to achieve those goals.

Chapter 4, "Recognizing Your Learning Style," examines the types of "knowing" that are most common to the traditional lecture-focused classroom and the alternative types of intelligence involved with service-learning. You will come to recognize the different types of learning and be able to determine which apply best for you and which are most comfortable.

Chapter 5, "Becoming Culturally Sensitive," includes comments from students who told us that learning about themselves and their reactions to others was one of the most powerful lessons of service-learning. This chapter includes reflection activities to examine your world views and attitudes toward others.

Chapter 6, "Identifying and Developing Service-Learning Skills," discusses the types of skills that facilitate a positive service-learning experience to maximize your educational goals.

Chapter 7, "Building Interpersonal Skills through Service-Learning Relationships," introduces you to basic skills to establish positive relationships at the service-learning site.

Chapter 8, "Understanding the Phases of Service-Learning," identifies the phases of service-learning from beginning to end, answering the question "What do I say and do after I say hello?" Because connections aren't made automatically, we offer practical suggestions for each of the phases of the service-learning process.

Chapter 9, "Getting the Most from a Service-Learning Assignment," guides you through assessment, evaluation, and reflection to help you determine whether you're getting the most from your service-learning experience. You'll learn how to gauge your progress and your personal and educational outcomes, as well as explore assessment tools that help you to monitor your service-learning project.

Chapter 10, "Reflecting on the Service-Learning Experience," focuses on the importance of creating bridges with the agency staff and the other service-learning participants.

Chapter 11, "Ending the Service-Learning Experience," shows you how to connect your service-learning experience with your future goals. We offer a goodbye plan to assess your personal growth, skill development, and achievement of course objectives.

Finally, the list of resources provides helpful references for students considering or engaging in courses that include a service-learning component and sources for material quoted in this book.

From Here...

Every person on this earth is a unique individual who has something to share with the world. As part of the learning process, it's important for each person to recognize his or her strengths and skills and accept that people learn differently. If you're not afraid to step beyond the ivory walls of your educational institution and venture out into the real world, service-learning can provide you with a valuable alternative form of education.

Learning and knowledge cannot be taken away from you. They are yours to keep. With the help of this book, we hope that you will be able to enjoy and fully participate in the service-learning experience.

CHAPTER 1

Exploring the Idea of Service-Learning

"I think that everyone in every major should be open and willing to experience service-learning. What is the worst thing that could happen? Maybe that you would learn something that would change your life? Isn't that the reason why we are attending college? To learn something—and hopefully that something would have an influence on our lives? ... It is an experience that I will never forget."

Anna

The introduction of this book contained a brief overview of the idea of service-learning. This chapter provides a more in-depth definition, includes several examples, describes the benefits, and addresses common questions you may have about service-learning.

What Is Service-Learning?

Service-learning is a form of experiential learning and teaching that achieves course objectives while meeting an identified community need. *Experiential learning* is often described by students as a hands-on, practical form of learning by doing something that helps them to understand what's in the books. But experiential education is not the only cornerstone of service-learning. Doing something to help your community through service is important, but what makes the service-learning experience is the time spent in self-reflection and class discussion about the way students have learned the class's subject matter through service. Simply put, the value of service-learning as a learning-by-doing teaching method provides students, faculty, and community people with these opportunities (Eyler and Giles, 1999, pages 7–12):

- Learning from experiences
- Linking personal and interpersonal development with academic development
- Learning and being actively involved in the process of social problem solving
- Increasing citizenship through social responsibility

But don't just take our word for it. A recent Nazareth College graduate, Megan, wrote about her personal and professional change as a result of a service-learning experience. Megan's reflection describes how each of the preceding ideas became her reality as she participated in a college service-learning project at a county prison. Read Megan's words to see how doing, learning, service, personal growth, and reflection come together.

Megan's Service-Learning Experience

When I was told that the service-learning was incorporated into the Crime and Detective Fiction class and that we would have "book talks" with inmates, I became excited about the idea. I am a "hands-on learner," and an experience like this seemed right up my alley. I actually had to talk the pro-fessor into letting me into the closed class because I really wanted to take part in the service-learning experience. I had no idea how this experience would change my life.

We had much preparation in our class with planning and discussions about our fears, assumptions, stereotypes, and prejudices. And we also learned the theory behind the idea of service-learning. I knew service-learning meant "hands-on," but I had never experienced service-learning before. We were told that there would be a direct connection between our learning in the class and the service that we provided. [The professor] explained that this would not be a community service experience and we were not meeting with the inmates in a way that students would act as the "teachers" and the inmates would become the "learners." My class assignments included the regular type of in-class activities, but also I was required to attend weekly meetings with our book club members (students in the class and inmates at the correctional facility), be prepared by planning before the book club meetings, [and] write journal entries about my experiences after the book club meetings. I found the reflection journal entries difficult to do because I was so excited about the project that it was really hard for me to put that excitement on paper. I liked it when my professor gave us journal topics because it was easier for me to work with the structure that he provided.

I remember thinking that I had no idea what to expect. I was only a little nervous, but mostly excited about the chance to work with a group of people who were totally different from me.... The first meeting of the book club went well, as did the rest of our meetings. I remember being floored by "how into" the books the inmates were. When we only had to read a section or two for class, as most college students do, we read just that. The inmates read far beyond the scheduled readings and were disappointed in us for not wanting to read more. They showed us up, for sure!

By the time our last meeting came around, both the Nazareth group and the inmate group were sad to be separated. With the exception of our clothing, it would be difficult to determine who belonged to which group. Our good-bye was a little different than those working with any other group. There was no celebration party or exchanges of hugs, instead we celebrated with congratulatory words for a successful completion of the project!

I grew so much as a student and person during this experience. I learned so much about myself and those around me. The experience totally broadened my horizons and made me not only a better student but also a better person. I learned what I needed to learn about Crime and Detective Fiction, but the biggest lesson that I learned from the inmates (and just entering and exiting the correctional facility) was how lucky I am to live the life that I live because I now know that with only one or two little changes, my life as a student and their lives as inmates could have been easily reversed. I learned that the people whom I thought were the most different from me (the inmates) were, with the exception of a few badly made choices, much like myself and so many people that I know.

In my career as a teacher, I cannot wait to incorporate service-learning into my classroom. What better opportunity might I provide my students than to give them an opportunity to practice/apply what they are learning? I think that it is so important that everyone has the chance to work with a wide variety of people in different situations and settings because when it comes time to get out into the "real world," diversity will be ever present.

Another student, Michael, made the connection between the reality of the hands-on experience and the course objectives:

> "A classmate's tears cannot be valued via a textbook. Nor can the ability to question oneself during the spontaneity of change ever occur from a book. We made decisions based upon what unfolded before us. We were not in the position to edit things as a book does. We faced and learned things by using all of our senses as the semester moved on."

The excitement Anna, Megan, and Michael showed about service-learning is meant to encourage you to take seriously the core ideas of service-learning:

- Service to others
- Connection with class subject matter
- Self-reflection of personal growth and awareness

What Are the Benefits of Service-Learning?

In each student's reflection, that student explained the value of a particular service-learning experience to him or her as a person, student, and future professional. The benefits of service-learning are unique to each person, each group being served, and each educational class. What you may learn from your service-learning experience in your social studies class while you participate in a voter registration drive may be a distinctively different experience from what a history class student who is engaged in archival assistance learns at a museum. At the same time, all service-learning experiences provide common benefits to their participants: students, teachers, and community partners.

Service-learning benefits students by

- Encouraging them to become more involved in their own education beyond reading a book, attending class, and taking a test.
- Increasing their awareness about their biases, prejudices, and stereotypes about others.
- Providing hands-on practical experience at an off-campus setting that introduces them to a new environment to learn new skills and meet new people.

- Providing an excellent resume builder and networking opportunity for career development and job hunting.

Service-learning benefits teachers by

- Providing opportunities to teach in a real-world manner that connects required educational content with everyday life.
- Creating a learning partnership among teachers, community members, and students so that each might learn from the other.
- Encouraging them to creatively address and assess student learning needs in a manner that responds to multiple intelligences and multiple ways of learning.
- Increasing their awareness about their biases, prejudices, and stereotypes toward others.

Service-learning benefits community partners by

- Giving them regular technical assistance to provide a needed service to the community.
- Allowing them to feel valued and appreciated for their community-based expertise and knowledge.
- Increasing their awareness about their biases, prejudices, and stereotypes about students and teachers.
- Creating a network with local schools, colleges, and universities to seek out additional resources and assistance.

Such benefits are common regardless of the educational course content, the community setting, the type of service provided, and the students' backgrounds.

How Do Service-Learning Partnerships Work?

Typically, service-learning courses are developed through discussions between a teacher and a community partner. The teacher knows the course objectives and the lessons students must learn to meet educational requirements, and the community partner knows of a particular need in his or her community. For example, the Nazareth College faculty combined service with learning to create these service-learning experiences:

- Anthropology and biology professors teamed up to create an eth-nobotany course in which their students learned about plant life as they created a brochure for a Native American cultural center.

- Music education students taught the fundamentals of reading musical notes and scales to children diagnosed with learning disabilities.

- Physical therapy students provided care to persons without health insurance at a local community health center.

- Students in a religious studies course learned about religion and the Holocaust as they conducted interviews with Holocaust survivors to add to the archives of a local Jewish community center.

- A professor in the nursing department partnered with a local community leader. Her students learned about health-care policy as they collected data for a local neighborhood association about the numbers of underserved people living in the poorest sections of Rochester, New York.

- A member of the social work faculty created a partnership with a local settlement house to teach her students about the early history of the social work profession.

- A theater arts professor's students performed plays for children who typically would never attend a live theater performance.

Although service-learning may appear to be a much better fit between the academic courses in the professional schools of health sciences, nursing, education, social work, and human services, service-learning also enriches the traditional liberal arts courses such as math, sciences, fine arts, history, and philosophy through civic engagement. The following examples of service-learning projects are taken from a wide range of courses:

- A group of students from an environmental economics class assisted researchers in gathering data about the Great Lakes region. Another group of students worked with a local environmental group.

- Building on their own interests, members of a nursing department made arrangements to complete their service-learning projects in areas that interested them. Sites included the Salvation Army, American Red Cross, local food pantries, nursing homes, and halfway houses.

- Students from a psychology class about aging interfaced with residents at a facility that cares for people with chronic health conditions. The students interviewed the residents and created a "portrait" of their lives. Many of these residents had few visitors and were unable to move around much. The residents looked forward to the visits from the students.

- As part of a diversity awareness course, students completed their service-learning experience with young people enrolled in an urban after-school program. This experience forced students out of their comfort zones. It encouraged them to interact with children that came from different cultural backgrounds.

You will find many additional ideas listed in "101 Ideas for Combining Service & Learning" at the Web site www.fiu.edu/~time4chg/Library/ideas.html. This Web site identifies different academic areas such as accounting, art, biology, business, liberal studies, and so on with a wide range of service-learning ideas.

How Is Service-Learning Different from Volunteering?

You may be wondering why all of this talk about service is so necessary. Why can't we just help people and not make such a big deal of it? This is a good question because providing service to others or helping someone might be such a simple idea. As children, we learn the value of sharing with others and the simplicity and ease of the idea of random acts of kindness from our family, our schools, and even bumper stickers! The idea of being there for others—whether it takes the form of lending your muscles to renovate a building, spending your time tutoring at a school, or being a friendly visitor to persons who are unable to leave their homes—is simple.

However, the way you offer service with a level of preparedness, skill-readiness, and ability to be self-reflective, thus *intentional service*, moves you to the next level of true giving of self to become more fully involved with the idea of service. For service to be intentional, your efforts need to go beyond your good will and good intentions toward others.

Service-learning is more than just helping out or doing a good deed for others and is not just a high school volunteer activity. To pull all of these ideas together, consider the following statement by Barbara Jacoby, a service-learning scholar (Jacoby, 1996, page 5):

"Service-learning is a form of experiential education in which students engage in activities that address human and community needs together with structured opportunities intentionally designed to promote student learning and development. Reflection and reciprocity are key concepts of service-learning."

Chapter 2 explores the differences between service-learning and volunteerism in more detail.

How Does Service-Learning Apply to Your Educational Experience?

Now that you have a better idea of what service-learning is, you may have several questions. Our experiences show that students who take a class that contains a service-learning component have several initial questions. These questions typically fall within the following topic areas:

- Definition of service-learning
- Connections between course content (theory) and the service-learning project (application)
- Comfort with multiple ways of learning academic material
- Uncertainty about what's expected from the student, including time, effort, and energy
- Fears about the grading process
- Lack of experience and performance anxiety related to conducting service activities
- Unknowns about the neighborhood, people, agency or organization, contact person, or level of guidance and assistance the student will receive

The bottom-line questions for students are a little more straightforward:

- What am I being asked to do?
- Why am I being asked to do it?
- How will I be graded?
- What will I get out of it?

Throughout the remainder of this book, we will answer these questions. For now, however, consider that questions raised by students at the beginning of the semester generally turn into statements of academic accomplishment and personal satisfaction by the end of the semester. "I learned more than I could ever learn from a book" and "I made a difference" are frequent end-of-the-semester reflections of students who participated in service-learning projects.

Let's consider some of the first questions and fears that you might have about your service-learning assignment. On the following worksheet, determine how you learn, and then list your thoughts and concerns about the advantages (pros) and the disadvantages (cons) of service-learning as a way for *you* to learn course materials. Your list of ideas will become your guide for a meaningful experience. Using it, you can accentuate the advantages that you listed and rethink what's necessary to turn the disadvantages into advantages.

Making Service-Learning Work for Me

Directions: Fill in each numbered item with a phrase that explains what factors contribute to your success as a student.

Some examples might include

...*I know what is expected of me.*

...*feedback and ideas are readily available.*

1. I learn best when _____

   _____

2. I learn best when _____

   _____

3. I learn best when _____

   _____

Directions: Based on what you wrote in the preceding section, review your thoughts and determine how service-learning can be an advantage or a disadvantage to the way you learn best. List those advantages and disadvantages in the space provided. Here's an example: If you learn best with clear instructions, a disadvantage might be that your instructions may be coming from the leader at the agency, not your teacher. If you work best with a team, then having lots of people to work with could be an advantage.

Advantages	Disadvantages
_____	_____
_____	_____
_____	_____
_____	_____
_____	_____
_____	_____
_____	_____
_____	_____
_____	_____
_____	_____
_____	_____

At this point, you should have a clearer understanding of the purpose of service-learning and what you can expect from your service-learning assignment. It's now time to pause, reflect, and write your thoughts and questions at this point in your understanding of service-learning.

Reflection: Where I Am Now

Directions: Read and consider each of the following statements. Then provide an honest response.

1. At this point, service-learning seems to me like…_____

    _____

2. Which makes me…_____

    _____

3. Because…_____

    _____

4. At the same time, the idea of service-learning causes me to…

    _____

5. So that…_____

    _____

6. Which will help me to…_____

    _____

7. But I still need to seek out the answers to the following questions…

    _____

8. So that I not only…_____

    _____

9. But also…_____

    _____

From Here...

In this chapter, you have begun to think more about service-learning, about the ingredients that help you to achieve success in your studies, and the ways service-learning might aid you in those goals. The next chapter starts you on the service-learning path. You'll explore the different ways of learning and teaching, and you might be surprised to find that your ideas about the goals of education need some revision.

Understanding the Fundamentals of Service-Learning

"The [service-learning] experience made me more aware of the needs of our community. I was not aware of how hunger affects so many people in our own community. As a nurse, the health issue of hunger crosses all boundaries and affects the health of our community. Children are especially the most vulnerable. I was surprised when I learned of how many children receive nutritional support provided by [the service organization]. I was able to interact and work with many different people with different ethnic and cultural backgrounds."

John

Being aware of your values, recognizing the strengths of others, learning with people who have cultural backgrounds different from yours, having a plan, and being willing to be flexible with that plan—all are components of service-learning because your energy is focused on service *with* people as partners, and not *at* people as objects of the service. Service-learning is a planned form of service that, in its design and intention, makes the connection between service with others and your educational goals and academic coursework. This chapter provides you with the basic information to build on your already existing willingness to serve, your good intentions toward others, and your educational goals. This chapter

- Shows you how the role of educational institutions is changing
- Introduces you to the principles of undergraduate education
- Defines a way in which you can be an active resource for your education and not just a passive recipient of traditional "lecture-centered" education
- Increases your understanding of service-learning as a meaningful way to learn subject matter while increasing your awareness of the importance of being involved with your community and the world around you

The Changing Role of Education in the Community

One topic of national conversation over the past two decades among scholars, policymakers, and community-based advocates is the need for high schools, colleges, and universities to become better citizens, contributors, and connectors with their local communities and the larger world community. Colleges and universities are being called upon by local and national groups, such as community action programs, justice organizations, and community organizations, to move beyond their isolated, walled-off classrooms with narrowly focused, self-serving students who are taught by intellectual experts.

This movement to extend learning beyond the high school or college classroom is crucial because the manner that a school, as a member of the local community, participates with its community neighbors may or may not build bridges. Think about it. How involved is your school with its local community? Does that myth of townies versus college kids persist where you live? Do folks in your town think that "those high school kids" are interested only in their MP3 players, car racing, sports, and dating? This disconnection between the community and the institutions of higher education creates walls of distrust and myths between those who are on and those who are off the campus.

To bridge this separation between educational institutions such as high schools and colleges with their community neighbors, school administrators are being challenged to join with different types of teachers—those who know and understand the beat of the streets outside the classroom. Superintendents, principals, teachers, college presidents, and professors are being challenged by local politicians and social activists to find community-based solutions to the persistent social and economic problems in their local communities and the country at large. Administration and faculty are being confronted to incorporate issues of social justice, civic education, and the enhancement of the quality of life for all people into their academic curriculum, educational objectives, and teaching methods.

Service-learning, as one way to join with the community, has been a major emphasis by community activists, service-learning scholars, and community-minded students. Service-learning is a way to strengthen partnerships and relationships between the educational institutions and community because service-learning encourages educational institutions to make changes within the classroom that reflect the reality of the world outside. Therefore, service-learning expands the idea from simply helping into citizenship participation and active community involvement.

Learning That Reflects Reality

Besides building partnerships between educational institutions and communities, service-learning experiences offer opportunities for students to be educated as well-rounded, community-involved persons. Service-learning provides educational opportunities for you to learn about yourself as a whole person, and not just as a student in a classroom. Through service-learning you will learn about yourself and others and will gain skills that will help you to become the professional you want to be.

Understanding the Real Reason for Attending School

Think about the reasons you chose to finish high school and attend college or pursue a certain career in the first place. No doubt you have been told that in order to get ahead, you need an education. So you might think that school is about getting an education to get a diploma in order to get a job so that you can get money to get a house, get a car, and maybe along the way get a partner/spouse and even get a family.

Well, the process of solely "getting" is no longer viewed as quality education. If an education isn't singularly focused on the "getting," what is the reason for attending school? Higher education is certainly focused on career and professional development. At the same time, a degree in history, accounting, or nursing provides a beginning set of educational tools. You need these tools so that you can

- Acquire and apply new knowledge
- Increase your skills for healthy living
- Be aware of the manner that your values and attitudes affect your relationships with others

High schools, colleges, and universities are being asked to move beyond simply providing a fundamental set of educational tools to incorporating living skills. When you graduate from school, it is important that you are not just ready for a career, but that you are ready for life as an ethical, honest, critically thinking, civic-minded, contributing person who cares for others.

Bringing the World into the Classroom

To teach students academic coursework that encourages civic involve-ment, education should be based on principles that speak to students' increased learning about citizenship and give students the necessary skills to more fully participate in community action. For example, the faculty at Indiana University–Purdue University at Indianapolis (IUPUI) developed the "IUPUI Principles of Student Learning" to define what they believe every graduate of their school should know:

- **Communication and problem-solving skills:** Students must develop the ability to write, read, speak, and listen effectively. They must also learn to use information resources and technology to be successful.

- **Critical thinking:** Students must develop the ability to analyze information and ideas carefully and logically from multiple perspec-tives.

- **Integration and application of knowledge:** Students must devel-op the ability to utilize information and concepts gained from stud-ies in multiple disciplines at school, work, and home. They should be able to demonstrate their knowledge and the way it relates to a problem or issue, especially given different situations.

- **Intellectual depth, breadth, and adaptiveness:** Students must show a thorough understanding of at least one field of study and must be able to compare the methods used in their field to the methods used in other fields. Students also should be able to modi-fy their academic perspective to fit various situations.

- **Understanding society and culture:** Students should recognize their own cultural traditions while gaining a broader knowledge and understanding of other cultures. It is essential that students understand the relationship that cultures and society have on the world as a whole.

- **Values and ethics:** Values and ethics play an integral role in the choices we make in life. Students should develop a sense of values and ethics to be able to make informed choices. The choices we make impact our personal and professional lives.

This list of principles shows that an education is not just a diploma or degree. These principles are consistent with the realities of the world of work and the qualities that are important to be a valued personal or professional partner. In our experience as human resource administrators charged with the responsibilities of hiring, training, supervising, and even firing employees, we agree that a high school diploma or college degree becomes merely a piece of paper if a person cannot demonstrate a range of personal qualities similar to the principles presented in the preceding list.

The Idea of Service-Learning Versus the Practice of Service-Learning

The principles described in the preceding section, which encourage the faculty's and students' active involvement to teach and learn the subject matter together, are also helpful to make the link between the *idea* of service to others toward the *practice* of service-learning *with* others. Because service-learning structures your learning out in the community, you have the opportunity to gain insight into the world outside your classroom through which you can gain the knowledge and skills to make a difference.

Let's look at an example. To fulfill one professor's course requirement, his Nazareth College students must serve meals at a local homeless shelter. If this activity were not part of a course requirement, it could be called "helping" or "service." However, in conjunction with this requirement to serve, this professor teaches students about the economic displacement of the local labor force, created in part by jobs leaving the Rochester area. He further teaches about the lack of adequate and affordable housing as a social problem and the lack of a livable wage. The professor and students discuss these sociological and economic issues, which contribute to the high number of homeless persons in the local community—and across the country—as a component of the class lectures.

In addition, the professor has students discuss their experiences and their reactions to their service at the shelter while he helps them to connect the reality of the lives of "those homeless people" with the issues of social and economic injustice. As students reflect upon their serving experiences, the professor guides them to explore their personal values and attitudes toward the homeless. Through reflection activities and the professor's encouragement, students learn the manner in which their personal beliefs have an impact on their level of involvement with people who appear to be so different. This is service-learning.

As Barbara Jacoby states in her book *Service-Learning in Higher Education* (Jacoby, 1996, page 1),

> "Service-learning is different than any other educational endeavors in that it can not happen within the confines of the classroom, a discipline, or a campus. By necessity, service-learning involves partnerships between the institutions and communities and affects students in multiple ways."

Components of Service-Learning

Service-learning exists when a credit-bearing course contains requirements for active involvement in a hands-on, structured learning activity. As identified in the example about the homeless shelter, service-learning incorporates experiential learning to help students make the connection between in-class learning and out-of-class life. This combination of community-based learning with theory (the knowledge building in the textbooks) and practice (the knowledge and skill building in action) provides students with a deeper understanding of course objectives. Service-learning has three main components (see Figure 2-1):

- Service with learning experiences connected directly to academic course objectives
- Reciprocity (which means equal say and power) between the agency staff and instructor to design, implement, and evaluate the service component
- Reflection by the students to document and gauge their personal growth, determine their achievement of course objectives, and provide feedback about their service-learning experience

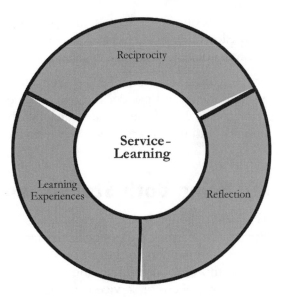

Figure 2-1: The three components of service-learning.

Service with Learning Experiences

The *Michigan Journal of Community Service-Learning* (2001, pages 12 and 13) defined service-learning as having these three important elements:

- **Relevant and meaningful service with the community:** Service that is both relevant and meaningful to all stakeholders must be provided in the community.
- **Enhanced academic learning:** The addition of relevant and meaningful service with the community must not only serve the community but also enhance student academic learning in the course.
- **Purposeful civic learning:** The addition of relevant and meaning-ful service with the community must not only serve the community and enhance student academic learning in the course, but also directly and intentionally prepare students for active civic participa-tion in a diverse democratic society.

Reflection: Making the Connection

The important connection between the service activity and personal learning is the structured reflection component incorporated into the course activities. Reflection may be in the form of class discussions, presentations, or journaling. Reflection opportunities may also include the faculty, students, persons being served, and program leaders providing feedback to each other about what is and isn't working in the service-learning experience.

In the classroom, structured reflections help students to examine their feelings, express their ideas, and ponder the bigger issues about the meaning of service, the reality of the social issues that they are witnessing in the community, and their own sense of contribution and civic involvement.

Reciprocity: Being Both Student and Instructor

In the best of the service-learning experiences, the faculty, students, and service recipients become partners in the process of teaching and learning. This partnership and relationship building is called *reciprocity*. Reciprocity is a vital component of service-learning because "reciprocity suggests that every individual, organization, and entity involved in service-learning functions as both a teacher and a learner. Participants are perceived as colleagues not as servers and clients (Mintz and Hesser, 1996, 36, cited in Jacoby)." Reciprocity occurs when the design of a service-learning project meets the teacher's course objectives and the community organization's needs because the teacher and agency staff worked together to determine the course's service-learning assignments.

The ability to build on each others' strengths becomes a basic ingredient in the service-learning partnership between community partners, teachers, and students. At first impression, a neighborhood or community-based organization may look disadvantaged to an uninformed faculty or student eye, or students may appear naïve and inexperienced to the seasoned agency staff who have "seen it all." However, through service-learning activities, each partner has the opportunity to move beyond initial impressions to build on the strengths of the other so that the roles of teacher and learner are shared.

How Service-Learning Is Different

You might wonder how service-learning is different from volunteer experience. Service-learning programs are designed to put together your academic and career goals with an education that informs you about your role as a citizen to be—at least concerned, if not involved—in the "bigger picture" of the social issues in your local community or social issues of national importance.

The following table shows the differences between volunteer activities, internships, professional field placements (such as nursing clinicals or student teaching), and service-learning. This table defines some of the differences that exist in various service or volunteer programs. As you review the table, notice that academic service-learning fulfills all three components: community service, enhanced academic learning, and purposeful civic learning.

Identifying Service-Learning Components in Other Activities and Programs

	Community Service	Enhanced Academic Learning	Purposeful Civic Learning
Academic Service-Learning: Connected to an academic course and offers course credit	Yes	Yes	Yes
Co-Curricular Service-Learning: Connected to activities offered through Offices of Student Affairs, Student Development, or Student Government Associations	Yes	No	Yes
Internship	Yes*	Yes	No
Volunteering or Community Service	Yes	No	No

* Not all internships involve service in the community.

As you learn to think beyond your own immediate needs as a student, service-learning experiences may help you to become more aware, concerned, and even moved toward activism related to community issues. You may begin to rethink your mindset from "why bother—it doesn't really affect me" to "I need to get involved and make change."

Through service-learning, students tell us that the terms *civic responsibility*, *citizenship*, and *democratic participation* have become more than memorized concepts in a political science, philosophy, or sociology course. Students indicate that they are now able to make a connection between their academic course requirements, the issues of social and economic justice, and their roles as self-aware yet community-oriented students and preprofessionals.

So how about you? In the following worksheet, take some time to reflect on various issues in your community, ways service-learning could expand your awareness of these issues, and ways your involvement will have an impact on your future career choices.

Connecting Your Social Awareness with a Service-Learning Experience

Directions: Read *all* of the sentences, and then write an honest response to each. It is important that you understand each question builds on the next as you think about your community and your role as an involved citizen.

1. Identify one social, one political, and one cultural issue in your community that you are aware of:

    Social: _____

    Political: _____

    Cultural: _____

2. Name a concern you have as a student that ties into these larger social, political, and cultural community issues.

    Social: _____

    Political: _____

    Cultural: _____

3. What might these concerns tell you about the assumptions and beliefs you have about others?

    _____

    _____

4. How might a service-learning experience build on your current awareness and help you expand your awareness?

   _____

   _____

5. Take a step further and reflect on the manner in which your involvement will help you grow into your future profession.

   _____

   _____

From Here...

This chapter demonstrated that service-learning is a tool that can be used to achieve common objectives found in any academic curriculum. At the same time, the design of service-learning is flexible in that its components can be customized to meet specific course content and objectives. We think of service-learning projects as educational "jump-starts" to stimulate your intellectual development as you grow into your role as a responsible citizen and ethical professional. As you learn to share what you have learned through structured written or oral reflection, you are better able to integrate the in-class theory with your off-campus practices and action.

The next chapter is designed to guide your thinking about not just your role as a student at a service-learning site, but who you are as a person making a contribution to others as you participate in your service-learning experience. We believe that successful service-learning experiences are not based on students' ability to have the "right answers" but based on students' willingness to be open, take risks, be dependable, and believe in others. How about you?

CHAPTER 3

Learning about Yourself through Service

"The resident's conversation with us strongly influenced me. I am scared of aging, scared of friends and loved ones dying, and scared of the unknown at times. She not only diminished these feelings but also actually made me look forward to some of what goes along with aging. I look at things from a different perspective. She taught me that it is possible to have a great outlook on life, be healthy, and still be independent in her old age."

Jennifer

Now that you have a foundation about service-learning as an idea, it's time to focus on you—not just what service-learning means, but what it means to you. This chapter guides you to connect with the idea of service-learning so that as a person, student, and preprofessional, you will be prepared for service-learning as a meaningful action.

Linking Self, Service, and Learning

In the preceding chapter, you learned that the three key components of service-learning are service with learning experiences, reciprocity, and reflection. In the following reflections from students, notice the linkage between self, service, and learning through service-learning and the increased knowledge and skill development. In particular, ask yourself these questions as you read the reflections from Yolanda, Shawn, and Joy:

1. What service actions did each student experience?

2. What did each student learn through his or her reflection?

3. How do you think each student's service actions and reflections helped her or him grow as a person, a student, and as a preprofessional?

Giving Back with Service-Learning

Yolanda wanted to be a part of the service-learning projects at her college because the opportunity gave her a chance to "give back" to her community. At the same time, Yolanda, who was taking a full course load, was worried about the service-learning time commitment because she had a part-time job along with her military obligations as a member of a local Marine Reserve unit.

Yolanda's Reflection

When I was young, there were people who showed me the way.... They took time with me, they helped me understand why it was important to do well in school. They helped me to have fun at the community center. And so I thought that by being involved in this service-learning project at the settlement house, it would give me a chance to 'give' to the kids the same type of attention that I received from the staff at the community center when I was coming up. When I was at the settlement house for my class's service learning project, I was a mentor with the kids. I listened to them talk about their day, I helped them with their homework, and sometimes we just sat and laughed about nothing.... As I reread my service-learning reflection papers for my class, I realized that at first I was nervous about the time commitment, but after reading over my reflection papers it is clear to me that I learned more about myself because of this project—my style of working with others, what I like and I don't like about working with others, and what it is like being a teenager today.

Yolanda's service-learning experience helped her to learn about herself as a future social worker who will work with urban kids. Her service-learning experience did require Yolanda to manage her time in a different way than studying for a test or writing a paper. She also told us that her stereotypes and prejudices of others changed. But most importantly, Yolanda gained a sense of commitment to her community because she played a small part in making a difference for the kids at the settlement house.

The Fear of the Unknown

Another student, Shawn, told us that his service-learning experience helped him to become aware of his reactions to "newness" with opportunities that were different from those he was familiar with.

Shawn's Reflection

I wasn't thrilled with the idea of service-learning because I didn't understand what was going to be expected of me or even what service-learning meant. I like to work by myself and not depend on anyone else for my grade in my classes. I am a hard-working student, and many of my classmates are more interested in hanging out and partying than completing their assignments. So, the idea of service learning at the Children's Hospital bothered me at first.

But once I got into the service-learning activities of doing artwork with cancer patients (which, by the way, I know nothing about) I realized that the newness of the project bothered me less each week because I looked forward to seeing the kids in the art therapy class. The kids, the nurses and I started to build connections—and I stopped worrying about the newness, what I didn't know about art therapy or kids with cancer— and I started to have fun! Not only did I learn something about working with children who have a life-threatening illness, but I realized, watching them, how I was so into myself. The kids taught me to reach out and live each day. I have many something news facing me ahead, especially as I try to figure out what my career goals are. So why not start now?

Shawn realized through class reflections that his initial dislike of trying service-learning was a feeling that comes up any time when he is asked to do something that is totally new to him. Through writing his reflection papers about his service-learning activities, Shawn realized that his dislike of something new affected decisions in different aspects of his life. This time, Shawn realized that there will always be something new in his life, and through service-learning, he began to move out of his comfort zone. Let's pause, reflect, and write in the following worksheet about the ways Shawn's reflection links self, service, and learning.

Linking Self, Service, and Learning

Directions: Review Shawn's reflection, and then respond to the following questions. Think about the links between Shawn's self, service, and what he has learned.

1. List Shawn's service actions (experiences).

    _____

    _____

    _____

2. What did Shawn learn (education) through his reflection?

    _____

    _____

    _____

3. From what you read, how do you think Shawn's service actions and his reflections helped him grow…

    …as a person?_____

    _____

    …as a student?_____

    _____

    …as a pre-professional?_____

    _____

Been There, Done That

Another student, Joy, initially couldn't understand the value of service-learning to her personal and professional development. Joy is very involved with on-campus and off-campus volunteer activities. She has been involved with some type of "giving to others" activities since she was in kindergarten because her family always stressed the importance of community service as a way to be a caring person toward others and a good community citizen. When service-learning was introduced as a course requirement, Joy told her teacher she had more than 15 years of experience as a volunteer in many different settings. Joy thought she was overqualified for the service-learning project, and she was concerned she would be wasting her time and money.

> "Why bother—been there, done that, so how could I learn anything new? I've been a camp counselor, I've worked in homeless shelters with my church group, our college's student association sponsors visits with the disabled veterans at the local VA that I attend once a month, and I am the vice-president of a college service organization. Why do I have to be involved in one more service project? What could I possibly learn?"

Joy's comments are typical of students who have a history of involvement in community service activities. However, Joy learned that volunteerism and community service are not the same as service-learning, as discussed in Chapter 2. Joy learned that the close interconnection of the service-learning activity at the Law Clinic with her prelaw course objectives, along with the structured reflection assignments, encouraged her to do more than provide a service to others. She learned that this interconnection of action and reflection—course work with service and self-awareness—stimulated her thinking about the criminal justice field and her reasons for choosing law as her future profession. As she spoke with the clients at the downtown Law Clinic, she was surprised by their lack of legal protection from sources other than the clinic, which was critically understaffed. Most importantly, Joy realized that learning is a life-long journey that may begin with one experience but rarely ends with another.

Joy's Reflection

I didn't realize how arrogant I was about learning and my education. I always thought of myself as being an open, adventurous person. But after I think about my first reaction to the service-learning assignment, and I actually thought that I had nothing new to learn, I am able to see how limited my thinking was about who I am and how I learn.

It was a real jolt when my teacher asked me: 'Is there anything that you can learn from this assignment if you think you have nothing to learn about working with people?' She really woke me up with that question. I mean, just because I will have undergraduate and graduate [school] completed doesn't mean that I will know everything that there is to know about being a skilled human service professional and working with all kinds of people. The most important lesson that I learned from service-learning was not one I ever expected—I really learned that I need to be open and flexible to all opportunities.

Personal Reflection

Now that you have had a chance to reflect upon Yolanda's, Shawn's, and Joy's experiences, it's time for your own reflection. Have you had any type of volunteer or service experience in which you learned something about yourself or your community? Did this service activity help you make a connection with your academic education? Using the following worksheet for your personal reflection, think about a service activity that did or maybe did not help you learn something like Yolanda, Shawn, and Joy did.

My Links to Self, Service, and Learning

Directions: Think about a service activity (or experience) you completed, and then respond to the following questions. Think about the links between self, service, and what you learned.

(continued)

(continued)

1. What service action (experience) did you complete?

   _____

   _____

   _____

2. What did you learn (education)?

   _____

   _____

   _____

3. Was there an opportunity for self-awareness and increased personal knowledge? If so, what was the opportunity, and what did
   you learn?

   _____

   _____

   _____

4. How did your service action (experience) and reflections help
   you grow...

   ...as a person?_____

   _____

   ...as a student?_____

   _____

   ...as a preprofessional?_____

   _____

Connecting Service-Learning Results with Educational Goals

Yolanda, Shawn, and Joy, like many students, state that service-learning experiences helped them to be aware of their inner world while they became more acquainted and involved in the outer world. Service-learning experiences help students acquire a greater sense of who they are as civic-minded, socially conscious persons, students, and pre-professionals.

A student who completed her service-leaning project at the Salvation Army says, "I am able to give back in a small way to my community and that gives me a renewed sense of purpose and belonging. On this Sunday, I made a difference to these people." Another student who spent his service-learning hours with the Red Cross states, "I contributed to the needs of the community and fostered my sense of my own civic responsibility. I have an understanding of the community that will help me when I graduate because I plan to live in this town."

Students also indicated that they increased or changed in knowledge, skills, and attitudes through service-learning activities. The following table illustrates the connection between the purpose of your education and the manner in which service-learning can help you achieve the goals of education, including those goals outside the academic component. The left column contains the principles of service-learning (from the *Michigan Journal of Community Service-Learning*, 2001, pages 12 and 13) stated in Chapter 2, and the right column contains the most common service-learning results experienced by students.

Connecting the Principles of Education with the Results of Service-Learning

Learning Principles	Students' Service-Learning Results
Relevant and meaningful service with the community	Increased knowledge about the subject matter
	Increased knowledge of community-related concerns and issues

(continued)

(continued)

Learning Principles	Students' Service-Learning Results
Enhanced academic learning	Written and oral communication skills
	Dependability and reliability
	Project organization and management
Purposeful civic learning	Ability to work with others
	Ability to recognize own strengths and limitations
	Sensitivity toward those who come from backgrounds and cultures different from their own
	Commitment toward creating a just society with a good quality of life for everyone

With this table, you can begin the mapping process needed to assess the personal qualities and skills you currently possess—and to determine the skills and personal characteristics that you would like to increase or enhance through service-learning.

Where Are You Now?

Before racing full steam ahead, take some time to reflect on where you are. When hikers go on a trip, they bring backpacks full of supplies so that they will have a satisfying journey. In this section, you will fill a service-learning backpack with the materials you need to make the most of your service-learning experience. You will list your strengths, create a statement of your personal strengths, assess your skills, and create a sample letter of introduction in order to prepare for your upcoming service project. Start by filling out the following worksheet to find out something about the personal strengths that you bring to the service-learning journey.

My Strengths

Directions: Using the table in the preceding section, determine the top five characteristics (from the column on the right) with which you feel the most capable and competent. List these characteristics in the left column, and then in the right column, list an example.

Characteristic	**Where and How You Put This Characteristic into Action**
1._____	1._____
_____	_____
2._____	2._____
_____	_____
3._____	3._____
_____	_____
4._____	4._____
_____	_____
5._____	5._____
_____	_____

Now that you have identified the characteristics you bring with you, it's time to create a Personal Strengths Statement. You can use this Personal Strengths Statement as a map indicating where you are now. Although your service-learning experience may be something new, you already have strengths that you bring to this experience.

My Personal Strengths Statement

Directions: In the space provided, finish the following statement:

The personal strengths that I bring to the service-learning experience

include... _____

_____

Which means... _____

_____

Because... _____

_____

Which will result in... _____

_____

Now let's think about the types of skills that you can pack into your service-learning backpack. The activities that you are involved with as a person and student, including your life outside school, have an impact on you in similar yet different ways because each activity requires similar but different skills and strengths. To fully appreciate how your current activities provide a foundation for your service-learning project, use the following worksheet to map out the skills you use or are gaining through those activities.

As you complete the following worksheet, consider different activities. Give examples of personal, school-related, and preprofessional activities. Include ways those activities reflect a skill that you currently demonstrate. Identify with asterisks those skills that would help you to be successful in your service-learning project.

My Skills

Directions: Determine the top five skills with which you feel the most capable and competent. List these skills in the left column, and then in the right column, list an example.

	Skill	**Where and How You Put This Skill into Action**

1. _____   1. _____

   _____   _____

2. _____   2. _____

   _____   _____

3. _____   3. _____

   _____   _____

4. _____   4. _____

   _____   _____

5. _____   5. _____

   _____   _____

Your backpack now has your Personal Strengths Statement and lists of your current personal strengths and skills. Based on your current strengths and skills, you can create a letter of introduction to your service-learning site supervisor. Using the following worksheet, write a letter of introduction that describes the qualities and skills that you bring to the service-learning experience. Don't be shy about highlighting your strengths.

My Sample Introduction Letter

Directions: Fill in the blanks, and update the appropriate items. You can also create your own letter of introduction.

Your Name
Address
Phone Number/ Email Address
Date

Name of service-learning site supervisor
Title
Agency Name
Address

Dear _____,

    The purpose of this letter is to introduce myself to you. I am a student in _____ class at _____ *(school/college)*. A component of my course requirement is to complete a service-learning activity at a local community-based organization. I received your name from _____, and I would appreciate an opportunity to discuss with you your agency's needs, my skills and interests, and the requirements of my class.

    I am very interested in a service-learning project with your agency because _____. I have skills in the areas of _____ that I think could be of benefit to the service-learning project. I also have previous work experience *(if not work, then mention volunteer experience or church involvement)* with _____. My previous work *(volunteer/ church)* experience has taught me the importance of _____, which may also be an asset that I bring to the service-learning project. I am excited about the possibility of learning more about _____ as I also make a contribution to your organization. I am available on _____ days from _____ to _____. I am required to contribute at least 3 hours per week for 15 weeks.

    I would appreciate the opportunity to speak with you in person about our goals for the service-learning project. I will contact you by telephone within the next week to set up an appointment.

I look forward to our working relationship.

Thank you,

Sign Your Name

What Are Your Values and Attitudes toward Service-Learning?

You have had a chance to assess your strengths and skills, but what are the values you bring to the service-learning project? What is your attitude toward service-learning as a part of your learning assignment for your class?

Recognizing your values related to service-learning is important. Although you may have personal strengths and skills, your values are what influence your willingness to learn and the appropriateness of your behavior for any given service-learning activity.

Yolanda, Shawn, and Joy represent three common types of student values/attitudes toward service-learning: the "I want to give back but how do I make it work" energy of Yolanda, the "Go-it-alone" philosophy of Shawn, and the "Haven't I already learned this?" hesitancy of Joy. Which reaction seems most like yours? You might even be feeling a little bit of each of these reactions. Using the experiences of Yolanda, Shawn, and Joy as a guide, complete the following worksheet.

Reflection: My Attitude toward My Service-Learning Requirement

Directions: Using Yolanda's, Shawn's, and Joy's reflections as examples, provide an honest response about your attitudes toward service-learning. Fill in your response to each of the following questions.

1. The "How do I make it work?" part of you says:_____

   _____

   _____

   _____

(continued)

(continued)

2. The "I like to go-it-alone" part of you says: _____

_____

_____

_____

3. The "What's in it for me?" part of you says: _____

_____

_____

_____

Another component of clarifying your values/attitudes toward service-learning is an honest assessment of your assumptions, concerns, and feelings related to your service-learning experience and the people with whom you may interact. Use the following worksheet to describe your initial reaction to the service-learning setting. What about the service-learning project reflects similarity/dissimilarity to your own background?

Reflection: My Attitudes toward Others at the Service-Learning Site

Directions: Yolanda, Shawn, and Joy shared that they had some pre-conceived ideas about the service-learning experience and the people at the service-learning site. In response to the following questions, write your honest assumptions about what you think you might experience in service-learning.

1. What are some of your assumptions about the service-learning

   activity?_____

   _____

   _____

2. The language of the participants?_____

   _____

   _____

3. The neighborhood where the service-learning experience takes

   place?_____

   _____

   _____

4. The racial/ethnic background of the residents?_____

   _____

   _____

5. The types of customs and behaviors of the participants involved

   in the service-learning project?_____

   _____

   _____

(continued)

6. The way that the service-learning participants will interact with

you?_____

_____

_____

7. The way that you will interact with them?_____

_____

_____

8. What do you hope your service will provide to the participants?

_____

_____

9. How might your service help make one small difference?_____

_____

_____

While completing this worksheet, you need to be honest and openly name your fears, concerns, and areas of comfort related to the service-learning setting. This way, you can grow from this awareness.

Where Would You Like to Be?

Your backpack is filled with your basic personal qualities. You have assessed your strengths and also demonstrated honest self-awareness in your discussion about your values, attitudes, and assumptions toward the service-learning experience, service-learning site, and service-learning participants. In this section, put together a map of what you would like to gain from the service-learning experience. Use the following worksheet to reflect on your strengths, skills, and values assessments. Use asterisks to identify the characteristics with which you feel the least capable and competent.

My Skill Development Road Map

Directions: In the left column, list five skills that you would like to improve, and then in the right column, list what you would like to learn.

Skill to Improve	**What You Would Like to Learn**
1._____	1._____
_____	_____
2._____	2._____
_____	_____
3._____	3._____
_____	_____
4._____	4._____
_____	_____
5._____	5._____
_____	_____

Finally, summarize your thoughts about the skills and personal qualities that you would like to increase. Consider also what you would like to learn through your service-learning project. Use the following worksheet to create your Personal Learning Goals Map. By filling in the blanks of the following statement, you will have the map you need to direct your service-learning experience.

My Personal Learning Goals Map

Directions: Using your responses to the preceding worksheet, finish the following statement.

The skills I would like to increase and the lessons I would like to learn through my service-learning experience…

Are…_____

_____

Because…_____

_____

Which means…_____

_____

With the hoped-for resulting effect on me…

…as a person:_____

_____

…as a student:_____

_____

…as a preprofessional:_____

_____

From Here…

By studying the student experiences and completing the worksheets in this chapter, you have a good foundation for knowing both where you are now and where you want to be as you begin your service-learning experience. With that in mind, turn to the following chapters, which use that information and guide you through mapping out the steps necessary to answer the question "What will it take me to get there?"

CHAPTER 4

Recognizing Your Learning Style

"I do feel service-learning is a valuable teaching strategy for future social workers. In my personal opinion, it is better to immerse yourself to see what it is really like out there. It is easy to read about something, but interacting is such a great learning strategy."

Miguel

What do you think of the way many states, school districts, and colleges emphasize test scores and grades? What do you think of the argument that, because test scores don't tell the whole story about a student's ability, your school needs to do more than just ask you to parrot back information? This chapter helps you examine your learning style and the methods of teaching that work best for your way of learning. In this chapter, we raise the questions: How do you know what you know? How have you learned? What have you been taught about the meaning of learning? What have you been taught about ways of gaining more knowledge and skills?

Teacher-Focused Learning Versus Student-Centered Learning

Your education may have been *teacher-focused*, or it may have been *student-centered*. What do we mean by these terms? Think about the classes in which you receive knowledge from the teacher. This type of learning is teacher-focused. Then think about those classes in which you are in a learning partnership—you and the instructor choose from various methods so that you can create your own path of discovery to knowledge. This type of learning is student-centered.

In a teacher-focused classroom, you come in, sit down, pull your notebook out of your backpack, and write notes based on a lecture given by the expert who stands at the front of the class. Notes on the blackboard, PowerPoint presentations, maybe some handouts, and straight lecture are the sole methods used. Little, if any, dialogue or discussion occurs among students or between students and instructor. You are responsible for digesting, memorizing, and repeating back the expert's words to demonstrate how well you understand and can apply the concepts. Many students are comfortable with this teaching model because the roles and responsibilities of knowledge-holder (teacher) and knowledge-seeker (student) are clear. Students who learn by listening (audio-oriented) and viewing notes on the board and then copying information (visually oriented) are comfortable with this teaching method.

In student-centered learning, your teacher uses many teaching methods—creative writing, videotaping, presentations, role-playing, drama, students as class facilitators, in-class small group peer tutoring, and off-campus experiential learning such as service-learning—regardless of the course content. Student-centered learning recognizes that everyone has a unique set of skills, attitudes, learning styles, and competence. The classroom has a give-and-take feeling, a flexibility between who is defined as the knowledge-holder and who is defined as the knowledge-seeker. Here, the environment makes it safe for the students to learn from the teacher, the teacher to learn from the students, and students to learn from each other. Take a minute to reflect on your most common educational experiences, and then complete the following worksheet.

Summarizing Your Learning Experiences

Directions: Read each question or task before you begin writing. Then write an honest response to each.

1. Describe to someone who has never visited your class what a typical day is like.

   _____

   _____

   _____

2. Describe your teachers' roles in most of your classes.

   _____

   _____

   _____

3. Describe your role as the student during most of your classes.

   _____

   _____

   _____

4. Are your answers for Questions 2 and 3 similar? Why or why not?

   _____

   _____

   _____

(continued)

(continued)

5. What do you do on your own so that you can learn the material presented in the class?

_____

_____

_____

6. What do your teachers ask you to do to prove that you have learned the material?

_____

_____

_____

7. Write one or two words that describe the teaching methods used in most of your classes.

_____

_____

_____

8. Write one or two words that describe what a teacher or teachers did that you really enjoyed and felt helped you learn the material.

_____

_____

_____

9. Are your answers for Questions 7 and 8 similar? Why or why not?

_____

_____

_____

10. If you were hired to serve as a consultant to your teachers, what advice would you give to them about the best way to reach and teach you?

_____

_____

_____

Your answers on the preceding worksheet may show that your most common educational experience has been teacher-focused. If so, you may think that the ideas presented in this chapter, as well as the service-learning experience, are strange because they are so different from your typical learning experiences. Or your answers on the worksheet may show that most of your education has been student-centered learning. If so, think about whether you are comfortable with that form of learning or you find it confusing. Which style of learning suits you best?

Multiple Types of Intelligence

Just as there are multiple styles of learning, there are multiple types of intelligence. Howard Gardner, who developed the theory of multiple intelligences, defined intelligence as "the ability to solve problems, or to fashion products, that are valued in one or more cultural or community settings" (Gardner, 1993, page 7). Gardner defined seven types of intelligences; he proposed that individuals learn differently, and that if students understand where their strengths lie and their teachers recognize those strengths, students can learn more easily. They also can remember what they learned for longer periods of time.

The following table outlines the seven intelligences as defined by Gardner (pages 8–9). This chart makes the connection between types of intelligence and examples of service-learning which reflect that intelligence.

Gardner's Seven Types of Intelligence

Intelligence	Description	Example
Linguistic	Ability to express one's self	You enjoy writing prose, poetry, journals, editorials, and so on.
Logical-Mathematical	Logical, mathematical, and scientific ability	You enjoy working with numbers and calculations. You may approach things very methodically, paying close attention to details. You are probably very good at problem solving.
Spatial	The ability to form a mental model of a spatial world and to be able to manuever and operate using that model	You have the ability to envision what things would be like in the future. You can view things from a broad perspective. You do not have a myopic view of things.
Musical	Strong musical abilities, as demonstrated by musicians, composers, and conductors	Music provides you the ability to express yourself. This expression can take the form of composing songs, writing lyrics, conducting ensembles, performing, or listening to music.

Intelligence	Description	Example
Bodily-Kinesthetic	The ability to solve problems or to fashion products using one's whole body or parts of of the body	You enjoy hands-on experiences. You learn best by being involved in the task or experience. This involvement can take the form of building or participating in the creation of something to simply expressing yourself or learning something through movement.
Interpersonal	The ability to understand other people—what motivates them, how they work, how to work cooperatively with them	You have the ability to communicate well with others. You are sensitive to others' needs and emotions.
Intrapersonal	The capacity to form an accurate, truthful model of one's self and to be able to use that model to operate effectively in life	You probably do a lot of self-reflection and enjoy working alone. You have a good understanding of your own abilities and how to use them effectively.

Gardner explains that very often a person has more than one form of intelligence, something he labels "plurality of intellect" (1993, page 9). Using the following worksheet, see whether you can discover your learning style and intelligence(s). Being aware of how you learn will help you as you progress in the service-learning experience. Aside from the academic skills necessary to complete a task, these learning styles drive how you handle yourself in different situations.

Discovering Your Learning Style and Intelligence(s)

Directions: For each intelligence, identify the activities you do well and those in which you would like to improve. You do not need to fill in all the blanks. Two examples are provided for you.

Intelligence(s)	Strengths	Areas of Opportunity
Linguistic	*Enjoy reading*	*Learn to write a play*
Musical	*Enjoy music*	*Learn to play a musical instrument*

Intelligence(s)	Strengths	Areas of Opportunity
Linguistic	_____	_____
	_____	_____
Logical/ Mathematical	_____	_____
	_____	_____
Spatial	_____	_____
	_____	_____
Musical	_____	_____
Bodily-Kinesthetic	_____	_____
	_____	_____
Interpersonal	_____	_____
	_____	_____
Intrapersonal	_____	_____
	_____	_____

Again, don't worry if you can fill in only a few of the sections on the preceding worksheet. As Gardner states, each of us is different. We each have different combinations of intelligences, and it is that combination which makes us unique. Remember Gardner's words (1993, page 12) to provide yourself with much open space to learn in different ways:

> "We are all so different largely because we all have different combinations of intelligences. If we recognize this, I think we will have at least a better chance of dealing appropriately with the many problems that we face in the world. If we can mobilize the spectrum of human abilities, not only will people feel better about themselves and more competent; it is even possible that they will also feel more engaged and better able to join the rest of the world community in working for the broader good. Perhaps if we can mobilize the full range of human intelligences and ally them to an ethical sense, we can help increase the likelihood of our survival on this planet, and perhaps even contribute to our thriving."

As you review the styles of learning and the multiple intelligences, think about the ways each style of learning can help you be successful in service-learning. Even if you aren't yet familiar with your service-learning site or are unclear about your responsibilities there, you need to recognize your wide range of intelligences to achieve your service-learning goals.

Using the following worksheet, reflect on each type of intelligence, and consider the ways the particular type of intelligence is helpful in service-learning. You might like to complete this exercise with a partner. Sharing ideas is a great way to learn something new.

Applying Multiple Intelligences to Service-Learning

Directions: Write down how each kind of intelligence is helpful in service-learning, and then write an idea of how you could improve in this area. You do not need to answer all the questions.

1. How can you use linguistic intelligence in service-learning?

    _____

(continued)

(continued)

2. How can you improve your use of linguistic intelligence in service-learning?

_____

3. How can you use logical/mathematical intelligence in service-learning?

_____

4. How can you improve your use of logical/mathematical intelligence in service-learning?

_____

5. How can you use spatial intelligence in service-learning?

_____

6. How can you improve your use of spatial intelligence in service-learning?

_____

7. How can you use musical intelligence in service-learning?

_____

8. How can you improve your use of musical intelligence in service-learning?

_____

9. How can you use bodily/kinesthetic intelligence in service-learning?

_____

10. How can you improve your use of bodily/kinesthetic intelligence in service-learning?

   _____

11. How can you use interpersonal intelligence in service-learning?

   _____

12. How can you improve your use of interpersonal intelligence in service-learning?

   _____

13. How can you use intrapersonal intelligence in service-learning?

   _____

14. How can you improve your use of intrapersonal intelligence in service-learning?

   _____

By completing the preceding two worksheets, you should find that you, too, have multiple intelligences. Although you may have more experience with a couple of intelligences, which indicates that you have learned to learn in certain ways, you can see that you have the potential to expand your way of gaining knowledge and learning course content through service-learning. Understanding how you learn best and integrating this knowledge with your service-learning experience will help you to have a more successful journey.

Multiple Stages of Learning

In addition to different styles of learning and multiple intelligences, there are multiple stages of learning. Using these stages, you can chart more than one way to complete your service-learning adventure that serves to reach out beyond your familiar paths.

One of the most widely known explanations of the stages of learning is Bloom's Taxonomy (see Figure 4-1). Based on education psychologist

Benjamin Bloom's theories of how people learn, Bloom's Taxonomy describes the process most people follow when learning something new. Unless you have been given the opportunity to work through the various stages of learning, you cannot get quickly to the point of being able to evaluate new material or a new subject matter.

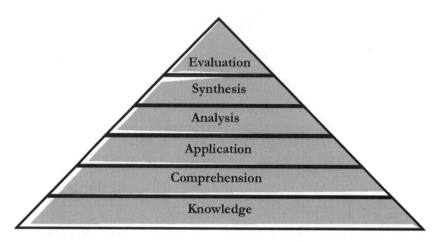

Figure 4-1: Bloom's Taxonomy.

Bloom believed that learning should be an integrated process, one that encourages you to apply the skills you have learned. Service-learning is an integrated process in that it encourages you to progress through the various stages from knowledge through evaluation. As you reflect on your service-learning experience, you will begin to see your progress through the various stages of competence.

To better understand the stages of learning, let's look at how Yolanda's understanding of service-learning developed as she progressed through Bloom's stages of learning:

- **Knowledge stage:** Yolanda understands that volunteering "is the right thing to do" for her.

- **Comprehension stage:** Yolanda learned in class that she would be completing service-learning, and her professor stated that service-learning was not the same as volunteering. For a few weeks, Yolanda pondered the difference between the two, but still she was unable to comprehend the definition of service-learning. She wanted to give back to her community, but she didn't understand the meaning of giving back through the service-learning process.

She shared her concerns with her professor and her classmates as she further tried to understand the difference. She also read the assigned chapters that explained service-learning. But the concept didn't "click" until Yolanda heard her professor say again and again, "Go to the people and learn from them. Don't think you have the only answers." Yolanda then had the "aha!" moment. She stated her comprehension in her service-learning log: "I get it now! I am not serving them to learn from them—we are serving and learning from each other!"

- **Application stage:** When Yolanda comprehended the meaning of the term *service-learning*, she learned to rethink her approach to her service-learning project. Instead of feeling overwhelmed because she thought that the success of the project rested solely on her shoulders, Yolanda applied the idea of "go to the people, learn from them," and "don't have the answers by yourself!" She felt more comfortable in the application of the concept of service-learning as she asked questions, accepted the fact that she didn't possess all the answers, and practiced her interpersonal skills to work as a group member.

- **Analysis stage:** Near the end of the semester, Yolanda took a step back to review her personal growth as well as her contribution to the service-learning project. At each stage of her learning, Yolanda examined her reflection journals, and she reviewed the feedback from her professor on her papers. Throughout this continual, semester-long process, Yolanda analyzed the skills she was developing and the attitudes that she was changing.

- **Synthesis stage:** Through her perseverance, self-reflection, and willingness to seek feedback from her classmates and her professor, Yolanda not only comprehended the difference between volunteering and service-learning, but she also brought together the purpose for service-learning with her course objectives. Yolanda combined her personal desire to give back to her community with her ability as a student to learn the course content through the service-learning experience.

- **Evaluation stage:** As Yolanda became aware of, comprehended, and tried out her new knowledge, she learned to evaluate what she was learning and what more she wanted to learn about herself, her coursework, and her professional goals.

Reflection Suggestion

Using Bloom's Taxonomy, take the opportunity to answer this question: What stage am I at in my service-learning experience? Use the quote from Miguel at the very beginning of the chapter as a thought jump-starter.

The following table shows how Yolanda documented her learning while working with young people at a settlement house. Note that each learning stage has specific skills associated with it. (Some of the skills listed do not include personal examples.)

A Real-World Reflection on the Stages of Learning

Stage of Learning	Demonstrated Skills	Personal Examples
Knowledge	Observe and remember information	"The settlement house is located in a stressed, urban neighborhood. The kids walk here from school, or ride the city bus. The neighborhood is similar to the one that I grew up in."
	Recall dates, events, places	"Our service-learning goal is to help the youth with their homework and to be there to talk with them. We need to be able to help them with their math, English, social studies, and science."
	Be aware of major ideas	"I work one-on-one with a teenage girl."

Stage of Learning	Demonstrated Skills	Personal Examples
	Know subject matter thoroughly	
Comprehension	Understand information	"Most of the kids' parents work, so the center gives them a safe place to come after school."
	Find meaning	"These kids live in this neighborhood; it is their home."
	Adapt knowledge to new context	"The girl I've been talking with is interested in two things: doing well in school and wearing fashionable clothes."
	Interpret facts and make comparisons	
	Categorize information and infer causes	
	Predict consequences	
Application	Use information	"One girl has begun to talk to me about school and her dreams!"
	Adapt methods, concepts, theories to new situations	"It is great to be able to assist the kids with their homework."
	Use required skills or knowledge to solve problems	"I'm getting a good refresher course in algebra."
Analysis	Recognize patterns and organize parts	"We try to develop relationships with the kids, but they don't all come on a consistent basis."

(continued)

(continued)

Stage of Learning	Demonstrated Skills	Personal Examples
	Discover hidden meanings	
	Identify components	
Synthesis	Build on old ideas to form new ones	"The kids have dreams just like I did when I was growing up."
	Generalize from given facts	"I hope that my presence here gives the kids someone to look up to."
	Pull together knowledge from several areas	
	Predict, draw conclusions	
Evaluation	Differentiate between ideas	"This program appears to be beneficial for the kids. I think it could more effective if they were able to come on a more consistent basis. I wonder how we could provide the kids with transportation and school supplies."
	Assess value of theories, presentations	
	Decide based on reasoned argument	
	Assess evidence	
	Acknowledge subjectivity	

What will you learn about yourself if you reflect on your experiences the way Yolanda did? Using the following worksheet, take some time to think about what you have observed, experienced, and learned.

Identifying the Stages of Your Learning Experience

Directions: For each of the six stages of learning, include an example from your own life. Perhaps you are learning a musical instrument; increasing your athletic skills; or even learning the basic knowledge, skills, and professional attitudes related to your career choice. Maybe you are just beginning to learn about service-learning. If so, this puts you in the first stage of knowledge development. In another area that is familiar to you, try to apply your progression of learning through each of the six stages and each of the skills demonstrated.

Stage of Learning	Skills Demonstrated	Personal Examples
Knowledge	Observe and recall information	_____ _____ _____
	Remember dates, events, places	_____ _____ _____
	Am aware of major ideas	_____ _____ _____
	Know subject matter thoroughly	_____ _____ _____
Comprehension	Understand information	_____ _____ _____
	Grasp meaning	_____ _____ _____
	Translate knowledge into new context	_____ _____ _____

(continued)

Stage of Learning	Skills Demonstrated	Personal Examples
	Interpret facts and make comparisons	_____ _____ _____
	Categorize, infer causes	_____ _____ _____
	Predict consequences	_____ _____ _____
Application	Use information	_____ _____ _____
	Adapt methods, concepts, theories to new situations	_____ _____ _____
	Use required skills or knowledge	_____ _____ _____
Analysis	See patterns and organize parts	_____ _____ _____
	Discover hidden meanings	_____ _____ _____ _____
	Identify components	_____ _____ _____
Synthesis	Build on old ideas to form new ones	_____ _____
	Generalize from given facts	_____ _____ _____

Stage of Learning	Skills Demonstrated	Personal Examples
	Pull together knowledge from several areas	_____ _____ _____
	Predict, draw conclusions	_____ _____ _____
Evaluation	Differentiate between ideas	_____ _____ _____
	Assess value of theories, presentations	_____ _____ _____
	Decide based on reasoned argument	_____ _____ _____
	Assess evidence	_____ _____ _____
	Acknowledge subjectivity	_____ _____ _____

We hope that these activities have helped you not only understand the theories of Gardner and Bloom, but also to connect these theories into your own personal experiences. Using these worksheets as your tools to understand where you are in the stages of learning will help you to understand your style of intelligence and your learning style more clearly as you become more involved with your service-learning experience.

As you travel on your service-learning journey, it is important that you make the link between rigorous education and service-learning. While you are at your service-learning site, you will see that the connection between service and learning becomes more obvious when you recognize the different stages and formats of learning and gaining knowledge.

From Here...

In this chapter, we introduced you to theories about education, thus the focus on how you know what you know. Then we asked you to apply those concepts to service-learning so that you could associate what you know (knowledge) with what you do with that knowledge (skills). Knowledge, skills, and attitude are the vital maps to guide your service-learning journey, as well as your pathway to professional development.

The next chapter introduces you to the importance of awareness of your cultural beliefs and attitudes as you learn about the beliefs of other groups of people. Service-learning is a process of building relationships with others who may, or may not, live in a neighborhood like yours or think the same way that you do. Chapter 5 helps you to appreciate and celebrate the differences and similarities between your background and the background of your service-learning partners.

CHAPTER 5

Becoming Culturally Sensitive

"I think that everyone has different values and beliefs, whether they be culturally or morally instilled, and I think that the opportunity to see that [the different values] first hand was an important part of the service learning project in making the connection between classroom and real life."

Stacey

Service-learning extends the classroom into the community in a way that engages persons from a wide range of backgrounds and belief systems. These opportunities allow you to gain a perspective about life beyond your classroom or dormitory. Learning about your culture as you experience others' ways of thinking about their world and interacting with others on their turf are beginning steps along the pathway to becoming culturally sensitive. So doesn't it make sense that you might open your service-learning backpack to include some new skills? Just as you would carry a compass or map while walking through an unmarked forest trail, you need to possess and put to use certain service-learning skills to guide your understanding, behaviors, and attitudes toward others.

In the best-case scenario, cultural sensitivity emerges when human differences are celebrated instead of viewed with skepticism. Being able to behave toward others with cultural sensitivity enhances relationships—with people you know, people you would like to know, and people you have yet to meet. Furthermore, cultural sensitivity is the foundation of personal knowledge, skills, and attitudes needed to become educated persons, well-informed citizens, and civic-minded professionals.

Self-Awareness

To encourage culturally sensitive service-learning, you must begin with an understanding of self. Only through self-reflection and personal awareness can you begin to make the connection between your biases and societal prejudice and your reaction to unfamiliar situations at the service-learning site. When you begin to understand the values and belief systems of your own background and heritage, you can overcome your own fears and assumptions.

Student comments reinforce this connection between service-learning and cultural sensitivity. Take a moment to consider the following reflections from students who overcame personal biases and gained a greater sense of cultural sensitivity:

"I shouldn't judge people before I meet them, it is much better to be open-minded going into a situation. I learned a lot about my inner prejudices that I never knew I had."

—Anthony

"I thought that I was better than these kids....I realized that these kids are not any better or worse than I am. They showed me that there is something to appreciate in everyone."

—Emily

"I have personally had to work on my biases. The service-learning project allowed me to experience working with others and the diversity that exists in working styles and personalities. I have come to value that diversity, although it was, at times, challenging. What I once would have considered a fault in someone, I can now see an area for growth and learning. This project has taught me that everyone has something to contribute and the diversity amongst us should be valued and should be used as an asset rather than be seen as an obstacle."

—Katrina

"It was important for me to see a different view of other people and become 'cultured.' This was the perfect experience because we were meeting on common ground, not inmates and Naz college students, but all as members of the 'book club.'"

—Megan

We approach cultural sensitivity from a perspective that it is important to respect people as unique individuals while also recognizing their cultural backgrounds. Remember, there is no one recipe of interaction based on a person's age, gender, religion, race, ethnicity, levels of abilities, or sexual/affectional orientation. Although the Golden Rule may say, "Treat others as you would like to be treated," we believe that it is important to treat others as *they* would like to be treated. It is insensitive and inappropriate to interact with people of any background based on your own beliefs and assumptions about others' cultures. Instead, a better approach to the topic of cultural sensitivity is to first explore the culture that you are closest with—your own.

Even if you are thinking "But I don't have a culture," try to consider culture beyond the typical racial or ethnic identities. If you were raised in a small midwestern town with no connection to your immigrant heritage, or if you were raised in Louisiana's Bayou country, you have a culture.

As you become aware of your own culture, your cultural beliefs and practices become more identifiable. You are able to move from a perspective of ethnocentrism (being centered by your ethnicity) toward an appreciation of a world of multiple cultures, or multiculturalism. You move from "What? Not everyone eats macaroni and turkey on Thanksgiving?" to understanding that some folks eat food from their native country on Thanksgiving, and still others don't celebrate Thanksgiving at all. Learning about your cultural self as you identify your beliefs and behaviors in a situation or environment that is foreign to you is a vital skill.

Rules, Roles, and Realities

To increase your own cultural-sensitivity skills, keep in mind that your own perceptions and experiences are influenced by the unique factors in your life. Families have a cultural belief system that influences the way they hear, see, think, feel, believe, and act. Some of these belief systems are obvious, whereas others are subtle.

To understand your cultural mindset toward other groups of people, you need to reflect on the lessons you were taught, messages you were given, and behaviors modeled for you by your family. We define *family* in a broad way: Think of the people who had the most impact over a period of time on your thinking about groups of people unfamiliar to you or your family.

The following worksheet contains examples of various cultural belief systems. Review these belief systems, and connect these ideas with the belief systems that you grew up with. If you know your service-learning site, connect your family's belief systems with those of the service-learning participants.

Understanding My Family's Cultural Rules, Roles, and Realities

Directions: Read through the following cultural belief systems. Then, in the space provided, identify your family's belief systems, and connect these beliefs to those of the service-learning participants. If possible, focus your comments on the people represented at your service-learning site. For example, determine whether you will be interacting with people of a different ethnic or racial background, the elderly, people with different mental or physical abilities, or people from a different economic background.

What are my emotional, physical, or cognitive expectations of people who are different from me? What do I believe that people who are different than me should feel, look like, think, and be able to do based on race, ethnicity, gender, sexual/affectional orientation, levels of ability, and age?

My family's beliefs: _____

_____

_____

The beliefs of the service-learning participants:_____

_____

_____

_____

What are the duties, responsibilities, or privileges based on race, ethnicity, gender, sexual/affectional orientation, levels of ability, or age?

My family's beliefs_____

_____

_____

The beliefs of the service-learning participants:_____

_____

_____

_____

What are the rules about responsibility, dependability, and getting the job done the right way the first time?

My family's beliefs:_____

_____

_____

The beliefs of the service-learning participants:_____

_____

_____

_____

(continued)

ce-Learning

9

(continued)

How is language used, including tone of voice, loudness, and use of words?

My family's beliefs:_____

_____

_____

The beliefs of the service-learning participants:_____

_____

_____

_____

What nonverbal communication is acceptable to use? How close can you stand next to someone? Is eye contact appropriate? Do you use your hands to make a point?

My family's beliefs:_____

_____

_____

The beliefs of the service-learning participants:_____

_____

_____

_____

What are the expectations around time, scheduling, and punctuality?

My family's beliefs_____

_____

_____

The beliefs of the service-learning participants: _____

_____

_____

_____

What is the age and gender division of chores and work responsibilities?

My family's beliefs: _____

_____

_____

The beliefs of the service-learning participants: _____

_____

_____

_____

What are the values and world views about acceptance or nonacceptance of others based on race, ethnicity, gender, socioeconomic status, living situations, religion, or level of ability?

My family's beliefs: _____

_____

_____

The beliefs of the service-learning participants: _____

_____

_____

_____

(continued)

(continued)

What child-rearing practices are used, especially techniques of behavioral management and control?

My family's beliefs _____

_____

_____

The beliefs of the service-learning participants: _____

_____

_____

_____

What types of clothing are worn? What music is listened to? What family entertainment and family holiday rituals are part of this culture?

My family's beliefs: _____

_____

_____

The beliefs of the service-learning participants: _____

_____

_____

_____

What is the division of labor—who completes what household chores?

My family's beliefs: _____

_____

_____

The beliefs of the service-learning participants:_____

_____

_____

These variations of values and expectations—roles, rules, and reality—change based on the family's beliefs about who can and who can't or who should or who shouldn't as they relate to issues of gender, race, ethnicity, and so on.

Just as family cultural variations have an impact on personal cultural upbringing, so do the realities of environmental, political, economic, and cultural events such as floods, war, civil rights, gay and lesbian movements, immigration, economic depression, famine, or corporate downsizing. These events may also have an impact on the values, worldviews, and expectations—again, rules, roles, and realities—of the different generations of your family. Consider the manner in which the Depression, the Vietnam War, the Gulf War, or the current troubles with unemployment or the war in Iraq affects different members of your family and their decisions about what is or isn't valued.

Let's put these concepts into practice. The following worksheet contains statements from students indicating that they entered their service-learning project with a set of values, a belief system, and preconceived expectations about the people that they would be engaged with. Complete this worksheet to identify their cultural values and expectations.

Identifying Cultural Values and Expectations

Directions: Read each of the following student reflection statements. For each statement, revisit the list of cultural belief systems, and then in the space provided, identify the cultural values and expectations. An example has been provided for you.

Student reflection statement: "I judged them before I met them thinking that they were going to be troublemakers. Yet when we did meet they were wonderfully mannered and fun to be around."

(continued)

(continued)

Value/expectation related to: __child-rearing, behavioral management__

What was learned through service-learning: __That she has expectations__

__about what is "mannerly" behavior and that she had biases against the youth__

__based upon their age, race, and neighborhood environment.__

"In the beginning I wanted very purposeful activities for each session, for the students to be involved and productive. Towards the end of the project, I adapted."

Value/expectation related to: _____

_____

What was learned through service-learning: _____

_____

"I will be the first to admit that until I participated in the service-learning program, I saw no difference in where you were raised. I thought everyone had the same type of choices for the way their lives turned out. I guess what I did realize was that there are not always choices."

Value/expectation related to: _____

_____

What was learned through service-learning: _____

_____

"I specifically chose this group because it challenged me in an area I've never been exposed to before. Overall I feel that I did a great job of not letting my biases interfere."

Value/expectation related to: _____

_____

What was learned through service-learning:_____

_____

Now it's your turn. Examine the list of cultural belief systems one more time, and as you do, reflect on your own values and expectations—your own roles, rules, and realities. In doing so, you will learn more about yourself, which will make it easier to relate openly and appreciatively toward others' cultural beliefs and practices.

Identifying Your Own Cultural Values and Expectations

Directions: Refer back to the worksheet on cultural belief systems, which you completed earlier in this chapter. In the space provided, list the top three items that you have a strong reaction to or feeling about. For each, write down the value or belief you have and the behavior you expect for that value or belief. Then write down your potential reaction if you approach this value or belief with celebration or with suspicion.

1. Value/Belief:_____

   Your value/belief statement:_____

   _____

   Behavior that you expect:_____

   Potential celebratory reaction:_____

   Potential suspicious reaction:_____

   Skills needed: _____

(continued)

(continued)

2. Value/Belief: _____

Your value/belief statement: _____

_____

Behavior that you expect: _____

Potential celebratory reaction: _____

Potential suspicious reaction: _____

Skills needed: _____

3. Value/Belief: _____

Your value/belief statement: _____

_____

Behavior that you expect: _____

Potential celebratory reaction: _____

Potential suspicious reaction: _____

Skills needed: _____

Based on this assessment, use the space provided to describe a cultural-sensitivity lesson that you might practice during your service-learning assignment so that you have a direction to become more culturally sensitive.

_____

_____

_____

Now, use the space provided to list five ideas to enhance your level of sensitivity, and list the action you will take to increase your appreciation of others' cultures.

Area of Cultural- Sensitivity Building	Action Steps to Take
1._____	1._____
2._____	2._____
3._____	3._____
4._____	4._____
5._____	5._____

Now that you have taken a first step to become culturally sensitive by reflecting on your own values and beliefs, it's time to get site specific. Prior to your first visit with the community partners at your service-learning site, take some time to learn about the setting and people you will be working with.

Relating Your Cultural Values and Expectations to the Service-Learning Site

Directions: Consider each of the following questions, and then write an honest response to each.

1. Have I ever been in this type of setting or environment before?

   _____

   a. What are my feelings about being at this location?

   _____

(continued)

(continued)

b. What can I do to celebrate the setting and environment?

_____

2. What are the characteristics that make the people that I will be working with different from me?

_____

a. What are the types of cultural differences that I need to be sensitive to?

_____

_____

b. What can I do to celebrate the differences in cultural beliefs, expectations, and behaviors?

_____

_____

c. Is there a need to decrease suspicion? What do I need to do to minimize my feelings of suspicion?

_____

_____

3. What are the common characteristics that I share with people that I will be working with?

_____

_____

a. What are the types of cultural commonalities that I can build upon?

_____

_____

As already stated, your own awareness is a very important first step toward becoming more culturally sensitive. After you have taken your own cultural "inventory," be sure to share your new self-awareness with your class instructor and your service-learning coordinator. Let them know the similarities and differences between the cultural rules, roles, and realities of your family and the service-learning site. Ask questions about the best way to be responsive with the people and the environment at the service-learning site. Like other students, you may be afraid to ask for clarification because you don't want to offend anyone. At the same time, a well-thought-out, truly concerned question isn't offensive; it's a question. Be an "askable" person who is willing to share information about yourself so that the cultural learning is a two-way journey!

From Here...

Remember, cultural-sensitivity skills require constant information updating, self-awareness fine-tuning, and self-reflection. Reaching acceptance and appreciation of others' cultural ways is a nonending process of growth and development. The energy and effort taken to become culturally sensitive are imperative in the process of building meaningful service-learning relationships.

Service-learning relationships are developed over a period of time and require additional skills besides cultural sensitivity. Chapter 6 highlights the phases of skill development as you travel on your service-learning journey. An array of skills that you may already possess, or that would help you with your service-learning activities, is described.

Identifying and Developing Service-Learning Skills

"Through the service-learning project, I learned that I need to step back and trust others. I also learned that I need to be more aware of my personal styles and how I can utilize my strengths better when I am working with others. While some of my skills were reinforced, I was also able to see where I needed some improvement."

Kristen

Service-learning and life in general become more meaningful when you understand that it is not just what you do, but most importantly, *how* you do it. Building how-to skills is a lifelong process, and the first step is to identify your abilities and skills so that you can strengthen them. To help you create a road map of your abilities and skills, this chapter identifies specific skills that are important to service-learning, everyday living, and any professional endeavor. In particular, this chapter focuses on three main areas:

- **The skill of identifying and celebrating the abilities and skills of the people you work with in service-learning:** Do you recognize and appreciate the fact that you can learn from other people, especially those you meet in your service-learning experiences? When you do, the depth of your learning and your ability to serve increase. This awareness, referred to as a *strengths-based perspective,* is critical in building relationships.

- **Skills necessary for service-learning:** The service-learning experience requires a very specific set of skills: cultural sensitivity, observation/engagement, communication, boundary setting, and project management. Remember, you will be developing, enhancing, and enriching these skills throughout your entire life.

- **Methods for developing skills:** This chapter provides some suggestions to help you continue with your skill development. The ideas provide you with an array of options to take your learning to the next step. These commonsense ideas have proven to be valuable choices for learning.

The best way to approach skill development is through a personal reflection on where you are now, where you would like to be, and what you need to do to develop service-learning skills. You began this preparation in Chapter 3, and now you are ready to take your skills backpack and road maps to the next level of awareness. Remember that the purpose of the exercises in this chapter is to develop awareness of your abilities and skills, not to judge them. The goal is to increase your self-confidence. If you are feeling brave, share your thoughts and ideas with someone you trust. When others share their feedback, ideas, and feelings with you, remember to remain sensitive and appreciate the differences.

The Phases of Skill Development

Skill development is just that, developing your abilities and skills over a period of time as you have new experiences, repeat old ones, and get feedback from other people. You may have several different feelings as you go through the various phases of skill development through service-learning. You will probably recognize that you experience these feelings whenever you learn a new skill, whether you're using a new computer, learning a new language, or conquering a new video game.

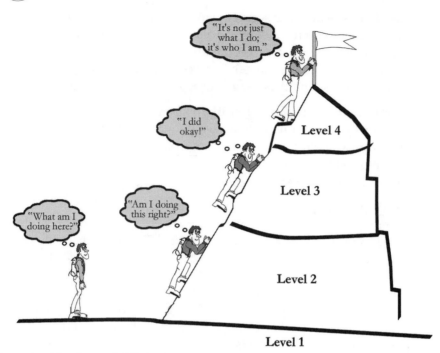

Figure 6-1: The phases of skill development.

Skill development consists of the following four levels (see Figure 6-1):

- **Level 1:** When you are in Level 1, you are just starting to learn a new skill in a new situation. You may hope and even expect to perform well, but then you realize that not everyone or everything is at the same level as you. You may feel *excited, frustrated, angry, or disappointed* because you have been asked to do something unfamiliar. If you have persistence and receive encouragement, you probably will keep trying, even though you may not feel as if you have mastered the new skill.

- **Level 2:** When you are in Level 2, you have been trying your new skills. You are learning to take deep breaths and think "small steps" each time you try something new. The situation feels less strange and more comfortable to you. At the same time, you really want to do the job right and yet be yourself. As a result, you might feel guilty or phony about the way you are approaching a new person, learning a new activity, or finding your way around the service-learning site. Recognize your feelings. Tell your instructor and classmates how you are feeling. Write your thoughts in your service-learning journal. Above all, give yourself credit for hanging in there!

- **Level 3:** When you are in Level 3, you have a sense of skillfulness. One day you walk into the service-learning site, and one thing after another seems to click for you. The days that you practiced your skills, reflected on your successes and frustrations, and asked for feedback and advice are now beginning to pay off. You feel much more confident in your activities, and the change is noticeable! Someone might even say, "You seem to be enjoying yourself here" or "I really appreciate your help."

- **Level 4:** When your awareness of your skillfulness becomes part of your sense of yourself, you have entered Level 4. Over a period of time, you realize that you have not just accomplished a new skill, but that the skill has become part of the way you think about and complete tasks, meet people, and approach life. Many students say they are amazed at the difference between their beginning and ending stages of service-learning. A common statement from students is, "Now I just jump into the task without worrying about looking stupid or doing something wrong." Someone else might comment positively about your approach to a new challenge or your interaction with a new person who could cause you to pause and say, "Gee, it's just the way I do things." When that happens, your skillfulness has become a part of your everyday actions and your abilities.

At this point, you are ready to assess where you are now with your sense of service-learning skill development. It is also important to think about your next step for skill development—where you would like to be. Use the following worksheet to complete this assessment.

Identifying Your Skills

Directions: Regardless of the length of time you have been at your service-learning site, identify one concrete skill you are developing or would like to develop. Then, for each of the four levels, write a sentence that reflects what actually happened (or is happening) to you as you developed that skill and what you felt (or are feeling) about what might happen while developing the particular skill.

(continued)

(continued)

1. Describe one skill you are developing or would like to develop.

   _____

   _____

   _____

2. Level 1: What am I doing here?

   _____

   _____

   _____

3. Level 2: Am I doing this right?

   _____

   _____

   _____

4. Level 3: I did okay!

   _____

   _____

   _____

5. Level 4: It's not just what I do; it's who I am.

   _____

   _____

   _____

Identification of Skills

"I do not take constructive criticism well. Noticing this has allowed me to work on this weakness."

—Allison

Identifying skills is a way to unleash your full potential! The following chart lists many skills that people have. Highlight or circle the skills you believe you possess. Also, feel free to write in any additional skills in the space at the end of the list.

advocate	empathize	organize
analyze	estimate	perform
assemble	evaluate	persuade
budget	explain	plan (logistics)
build/construct	facilitate	prepare food
calculate/compute	garden	present information
coach	help/assist	process data
communicate	improvise	recruit
compose/author	influence/persuade	research/investigate
conceptualize	initiate	repair
consult	install	sell
coordinate	interview	solve problems
counsel	instruct/train	supervise
create	manage	write
delegate	mediate	_____
develop	motivate	_____
edit	negotiate	_____

Now that you have identified your skills, use the following worksheet to create a formal skill inventory that you can add to your backpack.

Skills Inventory for Service-Learning

Directions: The following list of activities is an inventory of your skills for service-learning. Take time to review, reflect, and then record your skills.

1. Prioritize your list.

2. Trade your list of skills with a friend. Discuss the list, and see whether your perspective on your skills makes sense to your partner. In other words, does your partner think you have the same skills that you do?

3. Identify those skills you would like to gain or improve.

   _____

   _____

4. Develop a plan to gain or improve the skill.

   a. Can you accomplish this task on your own, or do you need help?

   _____

   _____

   b. How will you get the help you need?

   _____

   _____

   c. Set realistic goals and time frames for accomplishing these goals.

   _____

   _____

How Your Personality Interacts with Your Skills

The skills that you have will probably relate directly to your personality. For instance, if you are a very introverted, quiet, and reserved person, you might have difficulty talking to strangers. So, if communication is a skill that you would like to improve, you probably need to be aware of your personality as well. Understanding your skills and personality will help you as you make the most of your service-learning experience.

> "I was able to see what shortcomings that I had and what I needed to focus on in order to enhance my ability to be an effective social worker. My urgency is not another person's urgency."
>
> —Joseph

Look at the following personality traits, and highlight those that describe you best. You don't need to highlight something in each row. Please note that this exercise does not reflect on the quality of your personality; it simply is intended to make you more aware of how you are most comfortable in your interaction with others. Feel free to write in any additional traits in the space at the end of the list.

Sensitive	Not sensitive
Detail oriented	Not detail oriented
Calm	Lively
Laid-back	Energetic
Passive	Aggressive
Independent	Group oriented
Positive	Negative
Optimistic	Pessimistic
_____	_____

Now that you have identified your personality traits, use the following worksheets to identify how those traits interact with your skills.

Connecting Your Learning Styles with Your Personality Traits

Directions: In Chapter 4, you evaluated your own learning style. In the space provided, compare your learning style to the skills and personality traits you have just identified.

1. Are you able to identify a pattern? If so, describe the pattern.

   _____

   _____

2. Do you like what you see?

   _____

   _____

3. Would you like to change or improve on some things?

   _____

   _____

4. How does your personality play a role in your service-learning project? What do you need to be mindful of?

   _____

   _____

5. What personality trait would you like to improve?

   _____

   _____

6. What motivates you to want to improve your skills?

   _____

   _____

Reflecting on My Skills

Directions: Use what you've learned about yourself to identify your skills and your level of confidence with those skills.

1. What skills do you possess?_____

    _____

2. What three skills do you do extremely well?

    _____

    _____

    _____

3. What three skills do you do relatively well?

    _____

    _____

    _____

4. Which skills would you like to improve?

    _____

    _____

5. How can you improve these skills?

    _____

    _____

6. How will you know when you have improved the skills?

    _____

    _____

Remember that skills learned at a service-learning site are typically not some major force with a huge neon sign that blinks on and off and states, "Pay attention; lesson to be learned ahead!" Skill development occurs in a more subtle, consistent manner. Skill development takes time, and the learning may be subtle.

Some skills may be technical or educational in nature. Perhaps you developed new methods for tutoring, or maybe you learned how to use a new computer program. Other interpersonal skills may be more social in nature. For instance, you may have developed a clearer understanding of another culture. Or perhaps you learned some important skills related to communication—that is, how to present yourself in front of people who are more mature and experienced than yourself.

Ways to Enhance Your Skills

Now that you are familiar with your level of skills that are critical to successful service-learning, you can begin improving those skills. The following sections take you beyond skill identification and describe the ways in which you can improve and enhance your skills.

Attitudinal Check-In

After you begin your service-learning experience, you need to pause periodically to "check in" with your attitude toward your service-learning assignment. This is the time to retrieve the goals and objectives that you set prior to your experience. Take some time to reflect on the goals you set, and determine how realistic they were. Analyze how you have progressed in achieving them. Don't be too critical of yourself, but be honest. If you find that the goals were unrealistic, don't be afraid to modify them. Goals should stretch your abilities, but they should also be attainable.

Next, determine where you are in the growth process. Make some notes of what you think you need to do to achieve your goals. Set mile markers—periodic points in the service-learning experience when you should pause and reflect on the things you have accomplished.

These periodic "check-in" reflections allow you to assess your knowledge of the situation you are working in. Reflect on those things you first experienced and the way your feelings might have changed over time. Try to think about how or why your feelings have changed. Do you have a better understanding of the environment or roles that people play? Has communication changed? Are you more aware of the role that communication plays in any organization?

Take the time to update your thoughts, feelings, concerns, and so on in your journal. Don't be afraid to discuss your feelings with your classmates or instructors. Service-learning generally provides students with opportunities that they would not normally experience. Talking and sharing your thoughts with others are very important. We all need to share the things we are feeling. You may be surprised to find that others are feeling or experiencing the same things!

Mentoring and Requests for Feedback

Service-learning provides opportunities to learn from, develop relationships with, and watch in action your service-learning community partners and the service recipients. The chance to seek new knowledge and acquire new skills from people with vast professional practice experience and volumes of life wisdom provides an education beyond the classroom.

Our students consistently say, "I learned more here than I ever could from a book." So, for you to benefit from the expertise at your service-learning site, be prepared to ask thoughtful, insightful questions. Review your reflection journals to see whether you notice any consistent thoughts, ideas, insights, and concerns. Be prepared with an agenda of items to discuss so that you can take advantage of the creative energy and practice-based knowledge around you.

Other Ideas

The following list includes other ideas for developing your skills:

- **Discussion boards:** Use the Internet to discuss the skill you are trying to develop or look for ways to improve your skills.

- **Discussion circles:** Meet with your classmates and discuss a specific skill, along with how and why you would like to improve it. As you share your experiences with each other, try to come up with solutions together.

- **Literature:** Research literature and/or journal articles that may provide some insight into the skill you wish to improve.

- **Courses:** Sign up for workshops, courses, lectures, or independent studies to hone your skills.

From Here...

In this chapter, you learned ways to recognize and develop the skills that you have and those that you would like to develop. Take time to recognize and celebrate the skills that you bring to the service-learning site, as well as the skills that you want to enhance or increase. Think of your skills inventories, attitudinal check-ins, mentoring and feedback requests, and skills development activities discussed in this chapter as specific survival tools to pack in your service-learning backpack. In the next chapter, we help you build on your knowledge of skill development with a discussion of building relationships. The most powerful personal growth and professional development for our students evolved from their relationships with their service-learning partners.

CHAPTER 7

Building Interpersonal Skills through Service-Learning Relationships

"I found that the service-learning project helped me to combine my questions about how to apply my in-class learning with my knowledge of texts to incorporate it with the experience of working with members of a population."

Alisha

Your ability to build bridges with others while you participate in activities to make a difference on behalf of a greater societal cause relies on a belief about the general strengths of people and a variety of interpersonal skills and behaviors.

This chapter highlights two major topics:

- An asset-based perspective to help you recognize and appreciate the benefits that service-learning partners bring to your experience

- Skills that help relationship building, such as the ability to identify and maintain boundaries, observation and engagement skills, and communication skills

Using an Asset-Based Perspective

"I was blown away at the responses that inmates were giving. Their attention to detail was superb, and they are very much equals in academics. They gave enlightening responses to discussion topics and asked some great questions."

—James

An *asset-based perspective* encourages you to "discover and detail the gifts, abilities, and resources of each individual, household, association, and institutions in the community" (Catherine Gugerty and Erin D. Swezey, page 99, as cited in Jacoby).

An asset-based perspective helps you to acknowledge that within the community-based organization and the service-learning partners exist the creativity, hope, and control to address the community's needs. Although the scholarly knowledge of the professor and energy of the students are supportive elements to address community issues, an asset-based perspective reminds us that the community and the service-learning participant, such as the inmates identified in the preceding quote, have the primary expertise and insight.

Focusing on assets and strengths becomes more than a way to think about issues when you put that perspective into action. As the first step to putting an asset-based perspective into action, you need to frame service-learning as a reciprocal learning experience. Recall that reciprocity means a mutual give-and-take exists both in the learning and in the service. Use the following worksheet as a tool to assess the potential for give-and-take.

Identifying the Potential for Give-and-Take at the Service-Learning Site

Directions: Read each task or question before you begin writing. Then write an honest response to each.

1. List an ability, personality trait, and motivation that you have to offer the service-learning experience.

_____

_____

2. List two qualities of each community partner that could offer you a learning experience.

   a. The service-learning site

      1._____

      2._____

   b. The service-learning coordinator

      1._____

      2._____

   c. The service-learning program recipients/participants

      1._____

      2._____

3. How do these qualities build on and increase the strengths that you bring to the service-learning experience?

   _____

   _____

When you put an asset-based perspective into action, you take note of the solutions, not just the problems that exist in the daily happenings at the service-learning site. Of course, people might forget schedules, an activity might be delayed because of lack of resources, or the plans may be totally scratched on some days.

When you focus on others' strengths, however, you put coping strategies into action to overcome problems. Instead of using energy to gossip, worry, or complain, you begin seeking solutions. You must determine whether the solution lies within you to advocate for a better organized service-learning project or whether you become part of the solution by being flexible and adaptable.

The words you use are key indicators of your ability to activate the strengths of others. By avoiding phrases such as "those people," "why don't they just…," "it makes absolutely no sense…," or the most damaging phrase, "they don't know what they're doing," you can use your asset-based perspective to translate a doubt into a learning experience. Use the following worksheet to identify whether you have an asset-based perspective.

Identifying an Asset-Based Perspective

Directions: Read each task or question before you begin writing. Then write an honest response to each.

1. Identify one doubtful or "yes, but" situation that has created a challenge for you during the service-learning experience.

   _____

   _____

2. Use the asset-based perspective to write a solution that you could put into action. Be sure to use positive language.

   _____

   _____

3. Identify at least two things you learned from this experience. Perhaps you learned from someone else?

   _____

   _____

Your willingness to see that "the glass is half-full" or that a silver lining exists in each experience will help you on your service-learning journey. That's not to say that it is okay for you to be exploited, manipulated, or treated poorly. It is NOT okay. Do not hesitate to alert your instructor and/or your service-learning coordinator if you feel uncomfortable or concerned about others' behavior toward you or if you feel hesitant about activities that you are being asked to participate with. Look ahead to the "what-ifs" listed in Chapter 9 if you have questions about your learning experience.

Finally, an asset-based perspective is based on being patient, being tolerant, being an active learner, and letting go of preconceived notions about what should or should not happen. As one student reflected, she has "a habit of getting an idea in my head of what I think things are 'supposed' to be like. And I get so wrapped up in that expectation that I miss how they really are. It's something that I need to work on."

Students who approach service-learning from an asset-based perspective demonstrate what we call qualities of "positivism/hopefulness." *Positivism/hopefulness* means that you are able to reach for and seek out the lesson to be learned in each situation by remaining open to all experiences as potential contributors to your personal and professional growth. Your positive/hopeful attributes help you to look for, be aware of, and stay alert to any new experience as a lesson to be learned.

In addition to a strengths perspective and personal qualities of positivism and hopefulness, relationship building requires the interpersonal skills of boundary setting, observation and engagement, and different types of communication. The next section introduces you to key interpersonal skills to build your service-learning relationships. Imagine these skills as food to nurture you on your service-learning journey.

Skill: Identifying and Maintaining Boundaries

"They [the adolescents at the youth center] are very close to my age group, yet I am placed in a position of monitoring their behavior. I find that I am not into this, but I also struggle where to draw the line of buddies. I don't know if this is the right word as a 'mentor.' It is all so confusing."

—Evan

Boundaries are defined differently depending on the type of service-learning setting, the purpose of the service being provided, and the professional monitoring guidelines. Boundaries can be the formal, professionally designated "lines drawn" that regulate professional behavior. For example, most human service professional associations, such as those that doctors, nurses, social workers, psychotherapists, and lawyers belong to, establish regulations around acceptable/unacceptable behavior—the boundaries between the professional and that person's patients or clients.

For example, confidentiality is one boundary reinforced by a regulation. Sharing clients' or patients' personal information without their written permission is not only inappropriate, but it is also unethical and illegal. So after a long day when people describe what happened at work as they sit with friends at a lounge or go out for dinner, discussing a client's or patient's case is wrong.

The same is true for you at your service-learning site. It is unprofessional and inappropriate to use names and discuss others' problems or issues in a casual, gossipy way. Discussing your learning at the service-learning site is one thing, but if you share personal information about clients, consumers, patients, or colleagues at the service-learning site, you are violating their rights for confidentiality. This sensitive and fuzzy issue requires very clear direction from your course instructor and community partner. Hospitals, for example, have very specific legal mandates about not discussing patient information, and you must abide by "mandated reporter" laws when you're working with children who appear to be either neglected or abused. Again, in this serious business, you need professional guidance from your service-learning coordinator and your course instructor.

Professional groups often set up boundaries to prevent dating and sexual relationships between professional and client, or to ensure the use of professional courtesy and language, or to guarantee that services purchased are properly rendered. Boundaries may not be defined by professional groups, but they exist and are often regulated in many settings. The following examples step over certain boundaries that may exist:

- Sharing personal information too freely; being friendly and showing your interest in developing relationships doesn't mean that you need to divulge your private information, nor would you seek out that information from others

- Driving people in your vehicle

- Working in a space outside your assigned area

- Completing tasks that are the responsibility of someone else

- Giving out your cell phone number or e-mail address to service recipients

- Addressing persons informally rather than using the formal salutation of Miss, Ms., Mrs., Mr., or Dr.

- Wearing certain types of clothing

- Making personal phone calls at the service-learning setting

- Failing to attend to paperwork in a timely manner

- Developing romantic relationships with persons at your service-learning site while assigned student responsibilities

- Accepting money or remuneration for your service-learning involvement

- Taking supplies in exchange for work completed

- Forgetting your role as a *student*—you are not a staff member, nor are you a parent, sibling, or a human service professional

When you are entering an unknown or unfamiliar situation, such as your service-learning site, having knowledge about the policies and procedures is smart and self-protective. Ask your instructor and service-learning partner to help you understand the boundaries. If they are not able to identify boundaries, you can use the preceding list as a way to discuss the expectations the agency has of you.

Understanding and respecting boundaries is an important component in the service-learning experience, and you need to become aware of these boundaries as quickly as possible. Prior to visiting the service-learning site, discuss expectations with your instructor. This is also a good time for you to raise any concerns or apprehensions that you might have. The following worksheet will help you to identify boundaries and any related concerns you might have.

Identifying Boundaries

Directions: Read each question before you begin writing. Using the preceding list as your guide, write your response to each.

1. What physical boundaries exist at the service-learning site?

   _____

   _____

2. What nonphysical boundaries exist at the service-learning site?

   _____

   _____

3. What issues do you need to be aware of prior to beginning your service-learning assignment?

   _____

   _____

4. What questions do you have for your instructor?

   _____

   _____

5. What questions do you have for your service-learning supervisor or placement agency?

   _____

   _____

6. Based on the population to whom you will be providing service, what are the boundary issues from the preceding list you need to be informed of?

   _____

   _____

Skill: Observation/Engagement

"By doing the service-learning as a group, I learned so much about everyone's skills and techniques of interacting with and advocating for the students. It allowed me to see different skills expressed, and I was able to learn new ways to approach a situation."

—Julio

Taking time to watch, listen, and learn from the surroundings of the service-learning site is vital to enhancing your knowledge of human dynamics and the process of social action. Because people are so often in a "get it done" mode, they forget to take the time to observe and learn from the people, processes, and practices in the place where they want to get it done. As a result, they often make quick and unsubstantiated judgments about the people and setting. We strongly encourage you to take time for nonjudgmental and strengths-based observation of the following items related to the service-learning site:

- **Aesthetics of the facility:** Signage, posters, decorations, brochures, level of care, and cleanliness.

- **Social interactions:** Staff with staff, staff with service recipients, service recipients with each other.

- **Styles of communication:** Soft, low-key or loud, aggressive, particular cultural languages being spoken.

- **Types of music and sounds in the facility:** What do you hear? Music from current hip-hop stations or songs from a bygone era or in a different language? Sounds of athletic equipment? Kids laughing? Adults yelling? People conversing? Or much silence?

- **Working styles of individual persons:** Are some people laid-back and easygoing when it comes to completing tasks? Are others hesitant to engage in social dialogue or take breaks during the task completion? Be aware of who goes with the flow and who is all business. Determine how you fit into either style.

Your ability to observe the activities at the service-learning site and then reflect on the meaning of these observations is a skill necessary for engaging with others. Megan tells us that she realized she needed to "teach myself to pay closer attention to what people are saying and the nonverbal information that I may be able to pick up from being an observer." Thus, with her closer attention to verbal and nonverbal communication such as body language, posture, and eye contact, Megan has a better clue as to how to engage with others. Engagement means participation, involvement, and interaction. Therefore, to engage with people, you need to understand their context—which means their reality and their environment from their perspective—not just your assumptions. Take a moment to consider Figure 7-1.

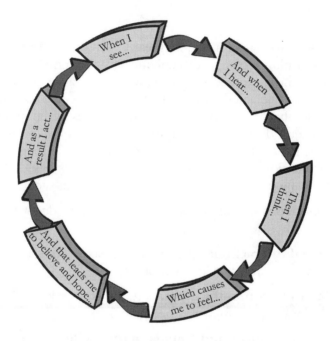

Figure 7-1: The Observation/Engagement Awareness Wheel.

You may find it odd to expect to accomplish service-learning goals without taking the time to observe and the opportunities to engage with others. Jumping right from seeing and hearing to behaving and acting without the benefit of self-reflection about your thoughts, feelings, hopes, and beliefs leaves you with limited opportunity to engage service-learning partners in a personally reflective manner. Again, taking the time for self-reflection reinforces the point of this entire book in that "doing" service-learning without reciprocity, relationships, and reflection is neither service nor learning. Whenever possible, we encourage you to work with your instructor and service-learning partner to incorporate dedicated time and structured opportunities to observe and engage with the site and its service recipients *prior* to completing the project tasks. Engagement takes place when you become actively involved in something. Engaging in a task, project, or discussion will inevitably occur while you're on a service-learning site.

Being enthusiastic is wonderful; being enthusiastic without taking time to observe and engage with others could be misinterpreted as ill-informed pushiness. Let others get to know you during the observation and engagement period. Use the following worksheet as a tool to observe and engage while you're at the service-learning site.

Observing and Engaging with the Service-Learning Site

Directions: Read each question or task before you begin writing. Then write your response to each.

1. Referring to the list about overstepping boundaries, choose three items you have observed. Describe your observation of each in nonjudgmental terms.

   _____

   _____

2. Describe the situation, location, people, and purpose of the observation/engagement.

   a. Using the Observation/Engagement Awareness Wheel, give one example of a recent observation at your service-learning site:

      When I see_____

      And when I hear_____

      Then I think_____

      Which causes me to feel_____

      And that leads me to believe and hope_____

      And as a result I behave or act_____

(continued)

(continued)

> b. What could I have done differently?
>
> _____
>
> _____
>
>
> 3. What skills do I need to be more successful with observation/ engagement?
>
> _____
>
> _____

You need to be aware of how you are acting and reacting in various situations. Be proactive in your assessment of your interaction with others. To do that, utilize the reflection process to ask yourself questions and reflect on your experiences.

Skill: Communication

"I learned the importance of good communication and how destructive it can be if everyone is not communicating honestly."

—Laronda

Communication—verbal, nonverbal, and written—is key to all aspects of a successful service-learning experience. Successful service-learning requires paying attention to each area because open and clear communication, whether face-to-face or written in an e-mail, is the glue that holds the experience together.

Through informal communication, you build relationships and establish social networks at your service-learning site. Through formal communication, on the other hand, you manage the service-learning project. Regardless of the purpose of the communication, you should remain culturally sensitive to the different ways of using words or addressing others by proper names. Additionally, you need to be aware of the tone and volume of your voice, as well as the tone and volume of other persons' voices. If you don't know the meaning of a term or concept, or what appropriate language or word usage is, be sure to communicate your concern.

Interpersonal Communication

By communicating your feelings of happiness or concern with language that supports your relationships, you can achieve your service-learning goals. Remember the saying, "It is not just what you say, but how you say it!" If you have a feeling or a concern, try expressing yourself by using an "I" message. In an "I" message, you use the word "I" to state that you have a feeling and that you take responsibility for that feeling and the need for a solution. This approach is less likely to create misunderstanding because the words "I feel…when…because" indicate that you are not blaming others for your feelings or situation. Here's one way you can state an "I" message:

I feel (name a specific feeling and remember the words *like* and *that* are not feelings)

When (a nonblameful description of specific behavior)

Because (how that behavior impacts you)

For example, here's how Shawn expressed one of his concerns at his service-learning site. On one particular day, Shawn observed some people who previously didn't want to work together; they were sitting together and discussing their assignment. Shawn remarked to his group members:

"I feel relieved…

"…When I see our group members talking and working with each other to complete the task

"…Because I don't have to take more of my time to make sure we get everything accomplished on time."

Because Shawn was able to share his frustrations with an "I" message, the open communication eventually led to finding solutions to the group's problems. On the other hand, if Shawn had used a "You" message, it may have increased group tension. Here's an example of a "you" message: "You are a jerk, and you make me angry because you don't follow through with your assignment, and you are a real slacker who shouldn't be a part of this group!"

Unlike a "You" message, an "I" message indicates that you have a concern that causes feelings for you, and you need a solution to the problem. A "you" message typically shuts down communication between people because it is blameful and judgmental, and it doesn't clearly state the problem. In short, using an "I" statement means that you recognize the potential that any issue is not one-sided and you share in what's taking place, as well as the solution.

Self-Reflection Communication

Another type of communication is related to the skills of self-reflection and self-awareness. These reflection tools and communication guidelines are more thoroughly discussed in Chapter 10. For now, note that your willingness to express your thoughts, ideas, and new learning in a non-judgmental, positive, strengths-based, and culturally sensitive manner during the reflection process is a cornerstone to your learning.

Task-Completion Communication

Another type of communication focuses on task completion. When you are discussing project management issues, using your relationship-building communication skills is important. You especially need to use a good, clear "I" message. At the same time, you can indicate the purpose of your communication as specifically related to the tasks at hand. Work with your instructor to determine and document expectations related to your tasks, including timelines. Also, discuss the manner in which you are to communicate with your instructor and service-learning partner about task completion. Make sure that your faculty, community partner, and you communicate and reach agreement about your goals, expectations, tasks, and scheduling.

After you establish mutually agreed-upon plans, it's a good idea to set up regularly scheduled meetings with your community partner so that you can communicate the progress of the experience. Also, agree on a process to use for communication outside any normal meetings to share ideas and concerns you might have. This type of communication may provide a great vehicle for reviewing goals and objectives. For example, you can use a form like the following one to update each other. Using this simple process allows everyone involved to express any concerns prior to any major problems occurring.

Reviewing Service-Learning Goals and Objectives

Directions: Define at least two of your service-learning goals. Then set up times to discuss these goals with your service-learning supervisor. Prior to meeting, write an honest response for each student perspective, and then discuss your supervisor's perspective at each meeting.

Goal #1: _____

Status #1–Date: _____

Student's perspective (Describe how things are going, what could be done better, what went really well, and so on):

_____

_____

Supervisor's perspective:

_____

_____

Goal #2: _____

Status #2–Date: _____

Student's perspective (Describe how things are going, what could be done better, what went really well, and so on):

_____

_____

Supervisor's perspective:

_____

_____

_____

Another way to track your communication or check in is to use a communications log. Tracking your communications accomplishes a couple of goals. First, it provides a diary of your discussions, one you can look back on for reference. Retaining this type of information will help you to see whom you've spoken with, what you've thought about during certain conversations, and also how you've grown. This type of log provides a reference of contacts and experiences you've had, and it provides an excellent source of information as you meditate and reflect on your service-learning experience.

Second, maintaining a log of communications may prove a valuable way of monitoring discussions and meetings. The following forms depict a couple of ways you might log the information. We encourage you to develop your own format, to reflect your own style of learning. Perhaps you prefer electronic versus hard-copy media to capture this information. Either way, the trick is to be consistent and to record the information on a regular basis. These two forms enable you to capture information that will be communicated throughout your service-learning experience.

Communication Log

Date: _____ Communication: _____

Notes: _____

_____

_____

Date: _____ Communication: _____

Notes: _____

_____

_____

Date: _____ Communication: _____

Notes: _____

_____

_____

Meeting Log

Date: _____ Location: _____

Agenda: _____

Notes: _____

_____

_____

Reflection: _____

Date: _____ Location: _____

Agenda: _____

Notes: _____

_____

_____

Reflection: _____

From Here...

In this chapter, you learned ways to take time to recognize and celebrate the strengths and assets that not only you, but also your service-learning partners possess. You also learned to recognize and develop the skills that you have and those that you would like to develop. Using this information, recognize the importance of the skills related to boundary setting, observation/engagement, and the different types of communication to build relationships, be self-reflective and manage your service-learning activities. Most importantly, take the time to learn and grow. Use your observations, reflections, and discussions to learn from your service-learning experience, and most of all, remember to have fun!

The next chapter describes the phases of service-learning so you can travel through the next stage of your service-learning journey.

CHAPTER 8

Understanding the Phases of Service-Learning

"What I learned is that meaningful things happen in ways that sometimes we do not see. So, now I know patience, and I understand that it takes time to make changes."

Vincent

Successful service-learning doesn't happen automatically; it evolves over a period of time. As a result, you go through phases of growing with your service-learning experience. We use the expression "growing with" because the entire service-learning experience is a *new* one—for you, for you *with* the community partner, for you *with* your instructor. You bring your own energy, personal wisdom, and goals to the service-learning project. Throughout the project, each of you grows *with* the other.

What have students taught us? After reviewing more than 150 student journals, we recognized a set of six phases that were common regardless of the course or site of the service-learning project. This chapter describes the different phases of the service-learning journey and offers concrete actions to make your transitions through that journey as smooth as possible. These phases offer a road map to acquaint you with possible detours and guideposts.

Phase 1: Pre On-Site Jitters

The pre on-site jitters phase occurs before you begin your service-learning project and before you go to the site where the service-learning project is being conducted. During this phase, students are introduced to the service-learning component of their course. Typically, service-learning, as a new, experiential way to learn, is an unfamiliar concept. Therefore, the idea causes students to experience a range of feelings. Many students describe some form of nervousness, ranging from apprehension to fear.

The reasons for the range of emotions are as varied as the actual feelings the students state they feel. For example, one student recognized her worry regarding her age and the age of the service recipients. She stated, "My biggest fear is the difficulty I may encounter with earning respect from the students because of our closeness in age."

Other students expressed concerns about the following issues:

- Leaving the safety of the campus.

- Entering unknown neighborhoods.

- Not being accepted by the service-learning partners.

- Not having enough directions or the right kind of information to achieve a good grade.

- Facing the unknowns, including questions such as What I am supposed to do? Who will help me? What if I make a mistake? When am I supposed to be there? How will I know if I am doing what I am supposed to do? Where do I park? Hang my coat? Put my book-bag? Why am I doing this?

Although some students may experience a sense of nervousness, others remain open to the new adventure with little or no expectations. One student, who participated in a book club with local county jail inmates, told us, "I tried to go into the first meeting of this project without any expectations other than to enjoy myself and learn from the inmates that I was going to meet."

Another student looked forward to becoming a "better person." She told us, "I have a feeling it will give us a little wake-up call and we will learn what we take for granted, hopefully making us better people."

During Phase 1 of their service-learning experiences, Yolanda, Shawn, and Joy thought about what they wanted to learn, how they would contribute to their service-learning partner, and how much time and responsibility they would have to expend. Each one approached the experience differently.

Yolanda began preparing for her experience by reflecting on her past experiences in volunteering. She recalled adults who were always giving up their time to make her life a little better. She knew she had a strong desire to give something back to the community. Yolanda understood that she was a bit nervous about the whole experience and the amount of time required. But confronting her fears with optimism helped her to overcome her nervousness and be successful.

After Yolanda began her experience, she took time to reread reflection papers she had written. From them, she could see her personal growth. Not only did she understand where she was mentally and academically when she began her journey, but she was now able to see the progress she was making.

Shawn was very nervous about the new service-learning course he was taking. He was an independent person and was unsure whether he could relate to the children and staff he would be working with. The key to his success was in identifying and recognizing his personality traits. He knew how he preferred to work and what would be expected of him. With this information, he could move forward. Often, we simply need to recognize certain traits that we have in order to work with or change them. Now Shawn looks forward to tackling the new things that arise in his life.

Joy had been volunteering for years and wasn't sure about becoming involved in a service-learning course. Throughout the experience, Joy learned the difference between volunteering and service-learning. She learned she had the ability to make decisions affecting her future career. She also realized the service-learning activities she was involved in had practical implications on her future career choices. Through the reflection process, she realized what type of personality and attitude she had and learned how to accept and look for opportunities to learn. Take some time now to consider any questions you have about starting your service-learning experience.

Reflecting on Pre On-site Jitters

Directions: Take a moment to reflect on any concerns you have prior to beginning the service-learning experience. Then write an honest description of these thoughts, or write down any questions you may have.

_____

_____

_____

A big part of the pre on-site jitters is the fear of the unknown. To overcome this fear, you need information. Use the following checklist as a guide to your own fact-finding mission.

Phase I Checklist

Directions: Review the following list, and check off the items when they are completed.

- ☐ Understand the beginning stages of the service-learning experience.

- ☐ Understand the structure and format of the course, the course outline or syllabus, and the service-learning activity.

- ☐ Have written expectations about your role as a student.

- ☐ Have clarification of the agency's or community-based partner's "do's and don'ts."

- ☐ Locate the creature comforts of the service-learning site: parking, a place to put your coat, bathroom facilities.

The first week on-site, students learn the proper directions to the service-learning location and gain a sense of comfort with the names and roles of the people at the site. After a couple of weeks on-site, students begin to seek out more information about the how-tos of the service-learning project that relate to achieving the agency's goals and easing their own nervousness. This is Phase 2.

Phase 2: Getting to Know You

The second phase described by students is a "getting to know you" phase that occurs during the first two to three weeks in class and on-site. During this phase, students begin to receive answers to some of the who, what, where, how, and when questions raised in the first phase.

In class, students describe this period as the time when they begin to interact with other students to share their excitement and ideas about service-learning. Typically, students complete their first service-learning reflection by writing down their assumptions, expectations, and fears about the service-learning project. They are encouraged to document the excitement or misgivings they have about their community-based assignment. Students share their ideas with one another and begin to rely on each others' suggestions to provide support and reassurance.

Students at Nazareth College who participated in a book club service-learning project at the local jail shared reflections about their first week on-site. One student told us, "We all enjoyed the first visit, it wasn't scary or intimidating; it was enlightening." An eye-opener for another student was "The steel doors still gave my heart a jump upon entering and exiting…not sure if I'll be able to kick this feeling, and the locked door is very bothersome."

Other students felt a sense of welcome when they entered the homeless shelter or the community center or the hospital because "the people were friendly" and the place looked "cheery and bright." On the following worksheet, reflect on your experiences in this stage of the service-learning project.

Reflecting on the Getting-to-Know-You Stage

Directions: Take a moment to reflect on the following questions. Then write an honest response to each.

1. Who have you met so far?

   _____

   _____

   _____

2. What are their jobs?

   _____

   _____

   _____

3. How do you react to the environment of the setting?

   _____

   _____

   _____

4. How do you feel?

   _____

   _____

   _____

In the following list, we suggest some agenda items for the first three service-learning sessions that are completed *with* (not *at, for,* or *by*) the students with faculty, students with faculty and community partner, and students with community partner and service-learning participants. Remember, you need to ease very slowly into any personal sharing discussions. You cannot assume that the environment is safe for sharing or that everyone has the ability to handle others' personal information. Also, be aware of the importance of confidentiality. Find out the details of the community-based partner's organizational policy related to sharing or discussing personal, confidential information.

- **Introductions:** Make the introductions fun. Maybe do some ice-breakers!

- **Strengths discussion:** Share ideas about areas of strength for students and community-based partners.

- **Special interests:** Review the special interests of each group, for example, faculty, students, community-based partners, and service-learning participants.

- **Working together:** What will each individual or group contribute so that the service-learning experience is successful?

- **Objectives and outcomes:** Review and understand the objectives and outcomes of service-learning for each partner member.

Phase 3: Does Service-Learning Connect with My Education?

After the "getting to know you" phase, students shift into a "does this really connect with my classwork?" phase during the third and fourth weeks. In this phase, students want the professor or instructor to provide a clearer connection between the service-learning project and their academic coursework.

Although some students quickly see the link between the service-learning project and their own personal and professional development, other students doubt the association between in-class discussions and out-of-class experiences. For example, several students in a Freshmen English Rhetoric course were skeptical that teaching the basics of story-book writing to young people who attend an after-school program would increase their own understanding of rhetoric. At the beginning of each class, the instructor conducted a 10-minute "check-in" with students to facilitate dialogue about the connection between the principles of undergraduate education, the course objectives, and the purpose of the service-learning activity. The instructor also invited the school's Director for Service-Learning and the Program Coordinator for the after-school service-learning project to listen to the students' ideas and concerns.

For some students, the connection was clear during the first week of the service-learning project; for other students, the link between service-learning and course objectives did not become clear until midway through the semester. As one student commented, "By attending service-learning, I have a better understanding of where they [the service-learning participants] are coming from, but also have the opportunity to reflect on my own values and beliefs and how they either assist me or inhibit me while working in a diverse society." What connection can you make between service-learning and your education?

Reflecting on How Service-Learning Relates to Education

Directions: Take a moment to reflect on the following questions. Then write an honest response to each.

1. How do you think this service-learning project relates to your course work?

   _____

   _____

   _____

2. Can you do anything to help make the connection?

   _____

   _____

   _____

Often this phase is challenging because the following questions arise: "What's going on? And who is in charge here?" You may question the commitment of the course instructor or community-based partner, the roles played by the various participants, the rules of the service-learning requirement, and whether the assignment is "stupid," "boring," or "a waste of time."

In this phase, attendance of the service-learning participants may become sporadic. During this time, both you and the service-learning participants need to be heard, acknowledged, and reassured. You may also need to refresh your memory about the skills for resolving conflict in a solution-focused and positive manner. Keep your eyes open.

This stage of development may provide opportunities for you (and the service-learning participants) to self-monitor your on-site behavior, your commitment toward the project, and your dedication toward learning. The following worksheet provides further ideas for making this phase successful.

Reviewing and Reflecting on Your Situation

Directions: Review each idea and then take time to reflect on it: Is this happening? Why or why not? How can you change things? Then, in the lines provided, write an honest response.

Constantly reinforce positive behavior and the range of learning opportunities to maximize what is working well.

_____

_____

_____

Gently invite and permit discussion about frustrations.

_____

_____

_____

Provide a forum for everyone to identify strengths, weaknesses, opportunities, and threats.

_____

_____

_____

Prepare yourself to work with others to determine solutions for the concerns that are raised.

_____

_____

_____

Reaffirm the course objectives and the goals for the service-learning experience with your instructor and the community-based partner.

_____

_____

_____

Discuss what it means to be a member of the service-learning project, and identify your own behavior that helps or hinders the progress of your own learning.

_____

_____

_____

Your commitment may waiver and your enthusiasm may become sporadic during this stage. To avoid having your discontent affect the other service-learning participants, use the following worksheet to explore your feelings.

Exploring the Reasons You Feel the Way You Do

Directions: Read each task or question before you begin writing. Then write an honest response to each.

(continued)

(continued)

1. Are the activities boring because you have not become fully involved in the project?

   _____

   _____

   _____

2. Is the climate/tone/environment of the host agency welcoming or inviting to you?

   _____

   _____

   _____

3. Has the mix of personalities of students and participants had an opportunity to "jell"?

   _____

   _____

   _____

4. Do schedules or transportation needs conflict with other activities?

   _____

   _____

   _____

5. Are you unclear how the course academic objectives have been fully infused within the service-learning planning and implementation process?

   _____

   _____

   _____

6. Are you being challenged to accommodate your individual needs for the sake of the entire project?

_____

_____

_____

Finally, keep these goals in mind as you work through this sometimes difficult stage:

- Take the time to get to know people, not just get something accomplished, because these stages build on your initial introductory and trust-building efforts.

- Strive to identify short-term, quick-success activities to facilitate your sense of connection. Your increased ability to complete even the smallest task and learning goal will help you to feel as though you are making a contribution and accomplishing educational outcomes.

- Share your concerns with your instructor or the community-partners in charge of the service-learning activity.

Most importantly, be aware of the impact of your own need for control, order, and sense of being in charge. Successful transition through this stage of development requires that you and service-learning project participants experience the developmental dynamics, so it is crucial for you to remain open to multiple ways to ask questions and resolve conflicts. Keep the faith!

Phase 4: What Does and Doesn't Work

After the "does it really connect?" phase, students evolve into a "what does and doesn't work" phase. In this phase, they give their opinions about the flow and organization of the service-learning project. By the fourth or fifth week of the project, student reflection statements move past "I don't understand what service-learning means or how it connects to my coursework" to "Why don't they just...." Students begin to make astute observations about the service-learning site and their interaction with service-learning participants. They reflect about their increased awareness of

- Their personal reactions to the people that they are (or are not) building relationships with

- The purpose of the service-learning project and the consistency between the hoped-for goals with what actually plays out on-site

- The available resources within the agency to meet its goals or specifically for the service-learning project

- The environment of the facility where the service project is conducted

- The connection between the course objectives and service-learning activity

- The roles and responsibilities of the different service-learning partners

- The behaviors that are helpful or a hindrance to building relationships and project development

In this phase, students' idealism about making grand social change is reexamined. The students are forced into the realism of making a difference one service-learning session and one person at a time. To do so, they must first look inside themselves rather than toward others. Thus, the students' reaction to the reality of the service-learning project is either one of celebration and applause or one of apprehension and critique.

The students' reactions depend on their own sense of preparedness for their participation with the service-learning project. The quality of planning, scheduling, and "working out the kinks" and the active involvement of and communication between the faculty and the on-site community person have a direct impact on their preparedness.

This phase is one of the most challenging for students. They are looking for quick results of their efforts to feel assured that they are not "wasting" their time or, more importantly, that the ups and downs of the service-learning project do not jeopardize their academic grade point average. Although students state this phase feels long-lasting, the phase actually quickly leads into the next phase in which students experience the "wow" connection. Using the following worksheet, describe your experience with what works and what doesn't.

Reflecting on What Works and What Doesn't

Directions: Take a moment to reflect on the following items. Then write an honest response to each.

1. List three things that work well with your service-learning experience and three that don't.

   _____

   _____

   _____

2. What would you do differently?

   _____

   _____

   _____

Phase 5: Now It Comes Together

"It is really amazing how many things you can learn about yourself by spending an hour a week there. I can't even begin to comprehend what I would take out of there if I were to spend more time."

—Evan

This statement is typical of students in the fifth phase of service-learning. About three-quarters of the way into the service-learning experience, students settle into and accept the successes and frustrations of the service-learning site's day-to-day reality. They no longer condemn the reality of change. Instead, they learn to be adaptive and flexible when service-learning plans are reassessed, whether the change is based on the needs of the community-based partner, inconsistent attendance of participants, or the contact person moving on to another job. With a sense of relief, students accept these regular occurrences in community-based settings as an integral part of learning rather than interference.

At the same time, students begin to recognize that such common community-based changes are infrequent events on a college campus where students' thinking is organized and scheduled around a course outline.

During this phase, students also move beyond critiquing and into a phase of "Wow, I am learning so much about me, my reactions, and my belief systems" outside the security of the traditional classroom setting. Furthermore, students become fascinated, rather than frustrated, by the lessons they are learning through making the "wow" connection between course objectives, reflection papers, class discussions, and their participation with their service-learning partners. What connections can you make about what you've learned?

Reflecting on What You Are Learning

Directions: Take a moment to reflect on each of the following questions. Then write an honest response to each.

1. What have you learned?

   _____

   _____

   _____

2. What makes more sense now than it did at the beginning of your project?

   _____

   _____

   _____

This phase leads to a sense of productivity, progress, participation, and pride. Like students who say "Now I get it!" you can now make a better link between the course content and the service-learning project. During this phase, be aware of what is working so that you gain a sense of your style as a partner and team member for the greater goal of service with others. Use the following worksheet to identify why you feel a sense of accomplishment.

Identifying Feelings of Accomplishment

Directions: Read each question, and then write an honest response to each. Think about when or why or how you feel a sense of accomplishment.

1. Do you feel a sense of accomplishment because you feel you belong?

   _____

   _____

   _____

2. Are you feeling competent in the skills you are using to achieve the goals you set?

   _____

   _____

   _____

3. Are you feeling as if you have some influence when you voice your ideas and suggestions?

   _____

   _____

   _____

4. Are you very active and involved so that you feel useful?

   _____

   _____

   _____

(continued)

(continued)

> 5. Do you see the connection between your efforts, the purpose of the agency, the course objectives, and the responsiveness of the service-learning participants to the activity?
>
> _____
>
> _____
>
> _____

Phase 6: A Good Good-Bye

Students are amazed by the quickness with which time passes to the end of the service-learning experience. "Before I knew it, it was over" or "Time just flew by after mid-term" are common statements. The last phase—"I made a difference, I learned so much, but how do I say good-bye?"—warrants much discussion. We devote most of Chapter 11 to saying good-bye, but here we summarize this phase.

During this last phase, students are able to talk about their sense of accomplishment. They recognize their increased self-knowledge, they gain a greater understanding of the course content than they had before, and they know they made a difference. Students genuinely feel a sense of contribution toward the greater goal of giving to others.

This sense of accomplishment doesn't diminish the simultaneous sighs of relief and regret that the experience is over. Students express a sense of relief because they now have one less academic obligation. At the same time, they feel regret because they are ending the friendly relationships they formed with community partners. At this point, students discuss the importance of a "good good-bye." Constructive closure is a key to bringing one service-learning project to an end while at the same time opening a door for the next group of students. What did you learn at this last phase of the experience? Complete the following worksheet to reflect on your experience.

Reflecting on Your Success

Directions: Take a moment to reflect on each of the following questions. Then write an honest response to each.

1. Do you think your service-learning project was successful?

   _____

   _____

   _____

2. Did you meet your goals? Why or why not?

   _____

   _____

   _____

3. What would you do differently?

   _____

   _____

   _____

This phase brings out numerous feelings in both students and service-learning participants. These feelings might range from "This service-learning experience was boring, anyway" to "I don't want to stop" to "I'll volunteer so we can keep meeting even though the class project stops." Separation can be an emotional time for all service-learning participants. The following ideas provide additional information for making this transition useful:

- In-class and on-site reviews of the service-learning achievements, lessons learned, and special times together provide an opportunity for students and service-learning participants to say good-bye in a positive way.

- A healthy approach toward termination allows clear and open discussion of expectations, accomplishments, and feelings.

- Although celebrations can take place throughout the project when special goals are achieved, the last session is also a great time to have a party with the service-learning participants. It is also important to identify the next steps after the service-learning project ends for each member as an important transition discussion.

- Do not make false promises about your future involvement. Many students have a difficult time with ending relationships so they ease their feelings by saying, "I'll be back." Don't say you will go back until you end your role as a service-learning participant and student. End your role as a student before you begin your role as a volunteer.

Think about the ways you can make your good-bye successful by completing this worksheet.

Thinking about Saying Good-Bye

Directions: Pause to reflect and write about ending your service-learning experience. Using the suggestions here, write your thoughts about how you will complete each step to say a "good good-bye."

1. Practice your skills to be able to recognize and articulate your feelings.

   _____

   _____

2. Acknowledge any and all successes, no matter how small. Remember, everyone wants to feel a sense of accomplishment.

   _____

   _____

3. Review your course objectives, look over your reflection journals, and evaluate what you have learned and what else you may want to learn.

_____

_____

4. Determine the appropriate methods and mechanisms to stay connected.

_____

_____

From Here...

This chapter covered the phases of development that both students and service-learning participants progress through. Think of all this information as another road map that you can include in your backpack. Just like any road map, this chapter provided you direction. We also caution you that sometimes there are detours, closed roads, and missed turns along the way. Service-learning is a journey—not just an end point. As you continue your travels, you continue to gain knowledge, skills, and values about yourself as a student, a preprofessional, and most of all, as a caring and involved person.

Chapter 9 offers answers about how to find a service-learning partner, how to become involved at your service-learning site, and how to appropriately respond to some potentially confusing situations.

Getting the Most from a Service-Learning Assignment

"Now, to me a sign of becoming educated is confusion, because the more I learn the more confused I am. I know that may sound strange, but this class has opened me up to seeing the world in a different light; whereas before I thought that I had it well figured out."

Evan

Your service-learning assignment occurs within a professional setting that has its own purpose, methods of doing business, service population, and daily operations procedures and processes. It is important for you to have an understanding or a road map of the organization's characteristics so that you are prepared to plot your direction of what to do when you arrive at the site. This road map builds on the discussion of the pre on-site jitters phase of the service-learning process discussed in Chapter 8.

In this chapter, we ask you to discover hands-on information about the community-based organization so that you are informed early on about the service-learning site's purpose, practices, and population served. Prior to your first on-site visit, we encourage you to understand the connection between the community-based organization, your course objectives, and your service-learning assignment.

This includes initiating a dialogue with your instructor (or the person who chose the partner) about the reason this organization was chosen as a service-learning partner. It is beneficial for you to understand his or her perspective. Why was the organization chosen, and how do its purpose, practices, and service-population provide the link between service-learning and your academic course objectives?

Choosing a Service-Learning Partner

If you are the person responsible for seeking out a community-based partner for your service-learning assignment, your ability to make informed choices about the partner you select can make or break the experience. Sometimes students make service-learning partner choices based solely on close proximity to the campus, the assumed level of safety of the neighborhood where the site is located, the types of people they feel comfortable with, or their familiarity with the type of service provided.

If you will be choosing the site, we encourage you to do some home-work about the organization prior to finalizing your commitment. Review the information in this chapter, visit the organization, contact the person in charge of volunteer recruitment, and speak with that person about your involvement with the organization. Be sure that person understands the difference between service-learning and volunteering and that you have specific course objectives you must achieve. Then make the decision about the fit between your academic needs and the organization's ability to work with you to meet its needs while addressing yours. After you make a decision, be sure to contact the staff person to let him or her know whether you are interested in completing your service-learning project with that organization.

Getting to Know the Organization

Regardless of whether you or your teacher chooses the community organization as a service-learning partner, it is helpful to have some basic information about the organization you will be working with. Use the following worksheet to identify the various components of the organization and to identify any other questions you may have. Having a better understanding of the organization can alleviate some of the concerns you might have upon entering a new situation.

Creating a Profile of the Service-Learning Partner

Directions: With the help of your instructor, the organization's Internet site, or the directories of the local United Way or the local Community Foundation, complete the following:

1. Identify the name, address, phone numbers, and contact information of the organization.

   Organization name:_____

   Address for placement:_____

   Internet site:_____

   Contact person:_____

   Contact person's title:_____

   Contact phone:_____

   Contact e-mail:_____

   Days and hours of operation:_____

   Purpose of the organization (possibly called the organization's

   mission statement):_____

   _____

   Types of services provided:_____

   Type of service that could meet your service-learning course

   objectives:_____

   Service population:_____

_____ © *JIST Life*

Age range: _____

Ratio of males to females: _____

Demographics (general overview of race, religion, ethnic back

ground, socioeconomic status): _____

General reason for the service population's participation in the

program or organization: _____

2. Does the service population participate on a regular basis at the
organization, or is the attendance sporadic?

_____

3. Will transportation concerns have an impact on the attendance of
the service population?

_____

4. What is the connection between your service-learning assignment,
your interests, and the type of service population's participation
with the organization?

_____

5. What are the strengths, skills, and competencies of the service
population? What might you learn from them?

_____

6. What can you offer the service population?

_____

Now that you have a basic idea of why the organization exists, where it
is located, and who it serves, use the following worksheet to trigger
ideas about how you might conduct your service-learning assignment.

Identifying Ideas for Conducting Service-Learning

Directions: Read each of the following questions. Then provide an honest response.

1. Will you be working indoors or outdoors?

   _____

2. Will you be working independently or with a group?

   _____

3. Will you be responsible for preparing activities? If so, who provides you with proper guidance to ensure the activities prepared are in accordance with the organization's goals?

   _____

4. Does someone at the service-learning site prepare the activities, and is your role to implement those activities?

   _____

5. Do you have advanced notice of what you are being asked to implement?

   _____

6. How do you make sure that you have the appropriate room? Resources? Supplies?

   _____

7. In addition to maintaining a strengths-based perspective and demonstrating cultural sensitivity, observation/engagement, communication, and boundary setting (as described in Chapter 5 and Chapter 7), what skills will you need? Consider the following types of skills, which may or may not be directly connected with your course content, and circle the ones you will need.

Tutoring skills

Recreation skills

Public relations skills

Human relations skills

Artistic, musical,
or athletic skills

Research skills

Public relations
skills

Advocacy skills

Information management
and technology skills

8. What resources will you need? And who will provide them? How
do you requisition the following resources?

Equipment: _____

Books: _____

Office supplies: _____

Computer: _____

Software: _____

Transportation for the agency participants:

_____

9. How will you get to and from the organization?

_____

Acknowledging Strengths and Assets

As discussed earlier, meaningful service-learning starts with an acknowledgment of the strengths, assets, and contributions each partner makes
toward the success of the service-learning project. Recall the idea of
reciprocity—the give-and-take between service-learning partners that

builds on each other's strengths to address each other's needs—as you take the time to learn about what makes the site what it is. Ask yourself these questions:

- What makes this site unique?

- Do the site employees have special skills?

- What is unique about the environment (building, equipment, resources)?

- How do the site employees interact and communicate with each other and with the service population?

- What tools do site employees and the service population use to communicate effectively?

- What do you, as an observer, like best about this service-learning site?

- If you were a participant, what would you like best about this service-learning site?

After you complete the profile of your service-learning partner, use the information to help you gain perspective about what you had expected from your service-learning experience. Review your completed Chapter 3 reflection about assumptions, fears, and expectations. Also, review your strengths and personal goals statements. Compare your initial reflections with your partner profile. Then consider what you might realistically expect based on this information. What do you need to adjust, change, or keep the same?

Identifying the Roles of Faculty, Service-Learning Partners, and Students

Important components of your service-learning journey are learning the fine art of beginning new relationships, understanding how to work with others, and navigating the various pathways to accomplishing a task. You need to understand the roles and responsibilities of the faculty, the on-site service-learning partner, and the students as service-learning collaborators.

To assist you in determining how these various service-learning collaborators complement each other to both maximize what you learn and complete a valued service, examine the following lists that describe who is responsible for what. Use this information to clarify the roles and function of each service-learning partner.

The role of the faculty/teacher is to

- Serve as the contact person from your college

- Oversee the service-learning project to ensure that students and the community partner's needs are being achieved

- Determine the academic requirements of the course, including course objectives, class schedule, required texts, course outline, and assignments

- Work in conjunction with the service-learning community partner/service-learning coordinator to develop service-learning assignments and a service-learning schedule

- Provide in-class orientation to the concept of service-learning and the educational benefits to students

- Mediate any major conflicts or problems that arise between the students and service-learning on-site staff

- Connect the service-learning experience to the academic subject matter through reflection activities in a regularly scheduled and consistent manner

- Review and provide feedback to students' service-learning plans, reflection papers, and service-learning evaluations

- Possibly make visits to the service-learning site

- Reinforce the importance of appropriate, legal, and ethical student and agency staff behavior

- Issue a grade for the course

The role of the on-site service-learning partner is to

- Serve as the community expert assigned to provide service-learning mentoring to students

- Provide overall direction for the on-site service-learning project

- Provide the on-site orientation, information, resources, and supplies to complete the service-learning project and activities

- Collaborate with the faculty/teacher to ensure successful completion of service-learning goals and students' service-learning goals in a way that is consistent with course objectives

- Provide students with information about community partner needs, strengths, and role in the community

- Assist students in making the connection between service-learning and service to the community

- Assist students with the implementation of the service-learning plan

- Possibly attend class to guest lecture about the service-learning site

- Possibly sign off on students' service-learning attendance sheet

- Directly confront students and contact faculty in the case of inappropriate, illegal, or unethical student behavior

Your role, as the student, is to

- Attend all classes

- Complete all written assignments by the assigned date and in the proper format according to the class outline

- Be active and proactive in your learning: ask questions, ask questions, ask questions

- Attend all scheduled service-learning activities

- Demonstrate professional and responsible behavior: punctuality, communication skills, positive attitude, accountability for assigned tasks

- Determine with the service-learning partner the appropriate dress for on-site activities

- Complete service-learning plans/work contracts, reflection papers, and evaluations according to due dates

- Remember the principles of higher education as your guideline for the range of learning opportunities; give yourself permission to think creatively and in a nontraditional way about achieving your educational goals

- Learn the policies and procedures of the community-based partner regarding day-to-day operations: confidentiality policies, sick-day policies, telephone usage, parking spaces, use of copy machines and computers, appropriate salutations of persons (how to address people)

- Be open and honest with faculty, staff, and on-site service-learning partners regarding learning needs and concerns

- Communicate problems or concerns directly with the person involved and let your faculty member know of your concerns; again, be an active learner and self-advocate

- Have fun and enjoy the learning opportunities

Discuss these different roles with your instructor and your service-learning partner. Is there agreement or disagreement about what can be expected from each other? Make sure that these roles are clearly defined in the beginning stages of the service-learning assignment.

Student-Identified Strategies for Success

The student reflection journals we've reviewed highlight other pathways to a meaningful service-learning experience, including on-site procedures, types of interaction, and increased self-awareness. Although these pathways are described individually in the following sections, it is crucial that you make the connection between achieving positive outcomes with the events that occur on-site and the kinds of contact you are involved with.

Some of the ideas listed here are consistent with the suggestions made in previous chapters about your approach to the service-learning assignment. The strategies listed in this chapter are the ones that Yolanda, Shawn, Joy, and other students identified most often when they identified qualities of a good service-learning experience.

You might think that the qualities listed here are not rocket science, but remember, more than 150 students from different academic disciplines indicated the same information. So, although the ideas presented may appear to be common sense, these ideas represent the practical wisdom gained through trial-and-error by the students who participated in service-learning assignments across a variety of academic departments. This type of wisdom not only makes for a successful service-learning experience, but also represents the foundational skills for personal development and professional growth.

On-Site Procedures

On-site procedures include those related to schedules, rules, goals, unexpected circumstances, and training. When faculty members, community partners, and students discuss these areas at the beginning of the assignment, there is more upfront coordination, which results in a more successful experience. The following table provides some suggestions.

On-Site Procedures

Procedures	Suggestions
Schedule	Develop a schedule that complements both your needs and the needs of the agency. Most importantly, remember that you are a guest at the agency. It is important that your presence there complements the agency's programs as well as your goals and objectives.
Rules	Gather, understand, and document the rules surrounding the agency that you will be working for. Be sure that you understand the rules your school may have regarding your service-learning experience. Examples may include security measures (wearing badges, signing in and out, being escorted to the site, and so on).
Goals	Set goals for yourself. Review these goals with your educational instructor, as well as the supervisor at the agency where you will be working. Be prepared to modify these goals based on the input you receive.
Unexpected circumstances	Be prepared to adjust your perceptions and expectations because dealing with unexpected circumstances is a critical part of the service-learning experience. Again, remember that you are the guest, and you need to adapt accordingly.
Training	Determine beforehand, if possible, whether the agency requires any specific training. Work with your instructor to ensure that you have the proper training to be successful.

Interaction

Interaction includes attention, praise, listening skills, observations, discussions, and responses. You might observe the mannerisms and models of interaction at the service-learning site in a nonjudgmental, culturally sensitive manner to learn about different styles of interaction.

- Remember that there are variations in the use of words, tone of voice, and verbal and nonverbal expression.

- Always ask questions to better understand the interactions of others if the mannerisms or approaches confuse you.

- Present your questions in a manner that indicates your interest in learning—for example, "Can you help me understand?"

- Consider that your question or comment may present an opportunity for others to share their own cultural background or the reason for a specific method of interaction at the organization.

The following table provides some suggestions for interaction:

Interaction	
Type of Interaction	**Suggestions**
Attention	Pay attention when you are on-site. Learn from those around you. Show your hosts that you are interested in learning and being a part of their agency.
Praise	Offer your praises to those you work with. In turn, you may receive praise as well. Look for the good in people and yourself. Don't hesitate to sincerely compliment others.
Listening skills	Use good listening skills, as part of the attention component. When people are speaking, listen well. Others will listen to you when you show that you are genuinely interested in hearing what they have to say.

(continued)

(continued)

Type of Interaction	Suggestions
Observations	Keep your eyes open. Watch those things that are happening around you. Among other possibilities, observe the physical environment, culture, and language.
Discussions	Take part in discussions. Express your interests, concerns, and successes with others. Learn from your classmates, teachers, and agency supervisors.
Responses	Be aware of how you respond to different situations; that behavior says a lot about you. When speaking with teachers and supervisors, be sure to listen first and then formulate a response. Try not to overreact. Be aware of your personality traits and those that you might want to improve or change. Use this service-learning experience as an opportunity to learn and grow in the way you communicate with others.

Self-Awareness

Students often express increased self-awareness as a result of their *active* participation in the service-learning assignment. According to the students we studied, their active participation in a variety of situations at the service-learning site was instrumental to their increase in self-awareness. Self-awareness ranged from improving self-advocacy skills, developing character, learning new social skills, and developing potential to helping self and others. Remember that earlier in this book, Yolanda, Shawn, and Joy shared their personal development as they reached out of their comfort zones to learn something new. The following table provides some suggestions to increase your self-awareness.

Self-Awareness

Skill/Concept	Suggestions
Self-advocacy	Remember that you are the one taking and paying for your course work. Continue to monitor your goals and expectations of the service-learning experience. When you have an issue or experience a problem, try to determine potential solutions. Advocate for yourself and those around you. But be sure that you understand your role in the situation and the facts surrounding it. Think before reacting too strongly.
Character development	Assess where you are, where you're going, and how you plan to get there. The service-learning experience is a wonderful opportunity to reflect on yourself, your personality, and the way you would like to grow. Take advantage of the feedback others provide you so that you can learn and grow.
Social skills	Keep in mind that many of us have a different set of social skills. Social skills are developed based on the environments we grew up in, the cultures we've been exposed to, and our general knowledge.

Be aware of your actions in different situations, and how others are responding. If you are confused, ask questions. Be polite when dealing with sensitive situations. Remember that you are the student and that this is an opportunity to learn and grow. Listen to the feedback others provide.

Use this opportunity to think about the career options you might have. Act in a professional manner. Show others that you are ready to move into the professional world. Be aware that people will assess |

(continued)

(continued)

Skill/Concept	Suggestions
	your readiness based on the way you handle yourself, the way you dress, and the way you speak and handle yourself in a variety of situations.
Helping self and others	Be prepared to help yourself, to explore new things, to gain expertise by using the reflection process. Make sure your agency knows that you are there to learn and to help.
Potential	Never underestimate your potential. Learning is a lifelong process. Take advantage of the service-learning experience to grow and to develop your full potential.

Dealing with What-Ifs

Up to this point, we have identified strategies to increase your readiness for active participation at your service-learning site. These strategies are based on practical wisdom and the lessons learned from the students at Nazareth College. However, the most significant strategy is your readiness to be flexible and adaptable to change when confronted by unexpected circumstances.

There always exist the unclear areas that we call the what-ifs. The remainder of this chapter includes examples of the most common types of what-ifs. Use them to acquaint yourself with unpredictable situations that students identified as tremendous learning experiences because these situations required here-and-now, reality-based answers. For your personal safety and to protect yourself against any misconstrued instructions or liability issues, we strongly encourage you to address the what-ifs with your faculty member and service-learning community partner.

Resource-Related What-Ifs

What if…

- **I find myself in a situation that requires administering first aid?**

    One of the first policies to find out from the service-learning site partner and your faculty contact person is the policy on first aid administration. Regardless of your own skills and level of first-aid readiness, there are vast legal implications if you administer first aid and you are not in accordance with the community partner's policies and procedures. *We encourage you not to administer first aid.*

- **I am asked by a service-learning partner to use my personal vehicle for transportation of others?**

    Regardless of your own willingness and driving skills, there are vast legal implications if you transport persons in your personal vehicle. *We encourage you not to transport anyone.*

- **I want to contribute my own funds for service-learning projects?**

    Determine at the beginning of the semester what resources are needed. If the resources do not appear to be available, discuss your needs with your faculty member and your service-learning partner. *We encourage you not to use personal funds for supplies or equipment.*

    Of course, it is probably appropriate if you want to occasionally bring a snack or treat to share with the people at your service-learning site or if you want to purchase small tokens of appreciation and thank-you notes. But, again, please verify with your service-learning coordinator. You need to be keenly aware of policies as well as the allergies children or adults may have.

- **The service-learning site is short-staffed and I am asked to help more than twice in an area outside my responsibility?**

    You are at the site to fulfill the requirements necessary to achieve the goals of your service-learning assignment. There will, undoubtedly, be times when you might be asked to help out with tasks different from those that you, your faculty/teacher, and the service-learning partner initially agreed on. Helping out the first time might be acceptable, and you might even enjoy it. However, after the second request for helping out, we encourage you to ask your faculty/teacher for assistance to stay on track with the original assignment—unless everyone renegotiates and changes the assignment.

Personnel-Related What-Ifs

What if...

- **I am assigned to a service-learning setting in which I am the minority person?**

  Being assigned to a setting where you are the minority person could trigger a wide array of feelings for you. This is an opportunity for you to identify and reflect on your feelings of being different to realize that "different" is not "less than." It is important for you to be willing to be open and discuss your feelings and ideas with your peers, your faculty/teacher, and the service-learning partner. This way, you can turn your feelings into learning experiences related to your undergraduate education.

- **One of my assignments requires assistance from the service-learning on-site partner who is very busy with his or her own responsibilities and rarely available to answer my questions?**

  An important component of service-learning is the cooperation between faculty, students, and community-based partners. Each partner must understand and agree to the expectations from the others. Although community-based partners may not be able to meet your every need at the instant you request help, it is appropriate for you to make an appointment to set aside time to answer your questions. Do not feel guilty about taking up their time, especially if faculty, community partners, and you have outlined far in advance the type of assistance and attention needed for you to successfully complete your project.

- **I don't like or I don't get along with another person who is a part of my class's service-learning project?**

  This is a common yet very serious concern raised by students. Typically, there is not one answer to this concern. Being able to constructively resolve disagreements and learning to understand a situation through a different perspective are highly valued interpersonal skills gained through a service-learning experience. Unfortunately, because some students do not have experience with positive conflict resolution skills, they can easily become bogged down in gossip and negative interaction that continues the problem rather than resolves it. Although some students say "I just ignore it" and other students say "I don't want to cause trouble," improving your ability to get along with others may just be the most important service-learning lesson for you. We suggest that you do not just ignore the situation, nor should you let the situation fester in negativity. Quickly seek counsel from your faculty/teacher. Don't wait! If talking to your faculty/teacher doesn't work for some reason, find someone who has experience in professional work environments and can offer sound words of advice. But seek resolution early! Remember to use an effective "I feel…when…because" message.

- **I am prepared for my service-learning activity, but no one shows up to participate?**

It is a working reality that the best of plans remain just that—the best of plans. There are always times when plans are let go due to lack of attendance or unanswered phone calls and e-mails, and what you thought would happen simply doesn't unfold in the manner that you had imagined. First, don't take the no-shows as a personal affront. Plans do or do not come to fruition for many reasons. Second, seek out your service-learning partner to determine if this could be a pattern and what your next steps need to be. Don't take it all on yourself to resolve the issue. Third, always reflect and inform your faculty/teacher of the situations that arise at the setting. And finally, see every circumstance as a learning experience— about how you handle frustration, what you are learning about the challenges of planning and implementation, and how you stay motivated to "stay in the game" as you let go of your disappointment or confusion.

- **I am offered an employment position or I would like to seek employment at the service-learning site?**

Employment might appear to be a natural next step for students who have found a good fit between their personal passion, professional interests, and the service-learning project. At the same time, ethical issues and boundary considerations become messy if you are employed by a service-learning site while you are a student in a class with a service-learning requirement. In the best-case scenario, your faculty/teacher and your service-learning partner-turned-boss are on the same page. In the worst-case scenario, your faculty/teacher and your new employer may view your role and responsibilities differently. Whose directions do you follow? How will your dual roles and responsibilities impact your learning and your grade? We strongly encourage you to seek guidance from your faculty/teacher before making a commitment.

From Here...

This chapter was devoted to the skills you might use to have a successful service-learning experience. We provided some practical exercises for choosing, identifying, and understanding your new service-learning partner.

This chapter provided sections on understanding procedures, recognizing types of interaction, and increasing self-awareness. This information is intended to help you grow—to help you be more successful. Now it's up to you to reflect on and take advantage of the suggestions. Finally, this chapter provided some practical examples of potential questions you might face and their solutions. The most important tool you'll need on your journey is communication. You can never have enough of it!

Throughout the chapters we have used the term *reflection* as a crucial component of service-learning. Reflection is what makes service and learning connect into service-learning. In the next chapter we explain that reflection is a skill and not just an assignment and describe techniques to help you develop your art of reflection.

CHAPTER 10

Reflecting on the Service-Learning Experience

"I learned that you have to be ready for change and be flexible to new ideas. I did a lot of reflective and critical thinking. The service-learning project helped me to relate the textbook to reality."

Selena

By this point, you are quite far along the path of your service-learning journey. The preceding chapters provided you with a conceptual framework to understand the goal, purpose, and outcomes of service-learning and to utilize concrete strategies to guide the successful completion of service-learning outcomes and course objectives.

To help you continue your journey, this chapter introduces you to the crucial concept that makes the difference between service-learning and volunteering or community service: the art of reflection. You'll add to your service-learning backpack the definition of reflection with examples of various styles of reflection activities.

The Art of Reflection

Joy, as you may remember from earlier in the book, was the student who had previous volunteer experience and was initially hesitant about the value of the service-learning project as just another volunteer experience. Joy's reflection demonstrates the importance of reflection as a way to be introspective and move toward a greater understanding of growth.

Sample Reflection from Joy

Without our contribution, the project would not be able to move ahead, and so another important lesson I learned is that small victories are still victories. Because I am my own worst critic and a recovering perfectionist, I often strive for 110 percent or nothing at all, but Sister Helen Prejean reminds us that it is 'better to help ten real hurting people—or nine, or one than to be overwhelmed and withdraw and do nothing (Loeb, 1999, p. 43).' By viewing my work as another step instead of the whole ladder, I am better able to put our contribution in perspective and see it as a success.

In my first reflection paper, I admitted that I intentionally chose the group I did in order to step outside my 'comfort zone of familiar classmates' and work with people whose styles definitely contrasted my own. I knew that by doing this, I would gain greater knowledge of my own interpersonal style than if I had simply joined a group that would help me get a good grade. And it worked! As I began, I knew that my need for control over my work would be difficult to give up; I also knew I would need to navigate the boundary between offending others in my quest for academic perfection and giving up those standards completely to avoid conflict at the onset.

You might ask: "Why should I bother to complete reflections on my service-learning experience? Don't I have enough to do without writing about my experiences and emotions?" In fact, reflections are a critical component of the service-learning experience. The primary objective of a reflection is to capture your thoughts and feelings about the service-learning experience. It encourages you to utilize critical-thinking skills to prepare for and learn from your service experiences. In doing this, you are better able to recognize the manner in which this experience interacts with and has an impact on the course for which it is designed.

In addition, the process of reflection encourages you to engage in a closer personal examination of your learning style, views of the world, assumptions, fears, and skills necessary to accomplish your service-learning experience. As you reflect on your personal awareness, you also have the chance to project your areas of growth and to achieve course objectives for the remainder of the semester.

Furthermore, reflection is the tool that captures and documents your thoughts and experiences. It provides you with an opportunity to connect your service-learning personal development and self-awareness with future professional goals. As we stated in Chapter 2, your reflection is what makes the connection between service and learning.

Connecting Reflection with Course Objectives

Effective reflection engages both teachers and students in a thought-provoking process that consciously connects learning with experience. Instructors play a vital role in helping students to focus on particular areas or to consider specific scenarios while reflecting on their experiences. One way that the instructors help students to focus their reflection process is to reinforce the course objectives as students reflect on their personal goals and objectives for service-learning.

By using clearly defined objectives, an instructor can enable students to focus their reflections. Taking time to reflect on these course goals, personal goals, and objectives makes the reflection process a rewarding and fulfilling experience. Remember to check the road map, or "work plan," that you developed at the beginning of your journey to use as your guide.

Reflections provide an unconstrained way for you to express yourself. The following sections provide some tips for completing a meaningful reflection.

Timeliness

People respond differently when asked to record their thoughts and observations. Some students jump right into the process of taking notes, documenting the poignant lessons learned or feelings felt after each service-learning session. Other students try to remember their reactions and feelings an hour or two before the reflection journal is due.

To make the connection between service and learning, you may find the best approach is to jot down notes and thoughts immediately after each service-learning experience. Doing so will make your reflection much more powerful because it will be more difficult to forget things that occurred. You can easily forget information and thoughts if you delay documenting the information.

Don't wait too long to capture your thoughts. Plan for and take time during or immediately after a service-learning experience to record notes and thoughts. Further, strive to meditate on your experiences and then, using your notes, complete the reflections using the agreed-upon format.

Sharing: How Much Disclosure Is Too Much?

To make the reflection a useful experience, you need to describe what you observed. You need to reflect on the people and situations that have occurred. You should make every effort to reflect on the relationship between the experience and the course objectives, discussions, and readings.

Whenever you write reflections, you should ask yourself, "How much disclosure is appropriate?" As we have stated in other chapters, care must be given to retain the confidence and anonymity of the agency and anyone you interact with. When writing reflections, try to be specific about your experiences and emotions, but be careful not to divulge too much information, especially if it relates to or can identify people.

Keep in mind the following guidelines as you write your reflections:

- Never use real names (for children, clients, or residents). Instead, use pseudonyms.

- Do not divulge specific information, especially if it was shared in confidence.

- Think about the positive side of a difficult situation.

- When you have critical thoughts, try to describe the situation in a factual way.

- Never reference or "attack" a specific person or group.

- Try to describe ways that you might have handled a situation differently.

- Reflect on why you feel the way you do.

Different Styles of Reflection

Reflection can take many forms: individual and group, oral and written, or directly related to discipline-based course material and not related. Reflection might include opportunities for participants to receive feedback from those persons being served, as well as from peers, teachers, and service-learning partners.

A well-designed format and feedback system ensures that reflections do indeed provide a valuable learning tool. At the same time, the format that you and your instructor agree on will work best when it reflects your personal learning style and technical capabilities. Both instructors and students may have learning and writing styles that respond more favorably to one of the methods described in this section. You can implement the reflection process in various ways.

It is important that professors and teachers provide quick feedback to students to encourage students to deepen their thinking and reflection skills and to encourage students to make the connection between class discussions and the service-learning experience. Be sure to use a reflection tool that allows for this interchange of ideas.

You can use a multitude of styles for your reflection. But regardless of which format you use to record reflections, it is very important that you apply critical-thinking skills to the process. Being able to synthesize and apply information encourages you to internalize the service-learning experience more fully.

How many notes you take is up to you as an individual. Be sure to take notes that you can decipher when you begin your reflection. Drawing or diagramming is also helpful sometimes, especially if you want to describe a room or setting. One helpful approach may be to begin each session with a question or an objective and then focus on that as your reflection. Your question may relate to a specific topic that was, or will be, talked about in class. Remember to relate your service-learning experience to your class content and theory discussions.

This section provides you with some questions that will help to stimulate ideas for the content of your reflections. You'll also find some examples of different reflection formats that are available. Most importantly, you'll get the opportunity to answer these all-important questions:

- Where am I?

- Where do I want to be?

- What will it take to get me there?

Thought Starters

To engage in the reflection process, you might need to use thought starters, as shown in Figure 10-1.

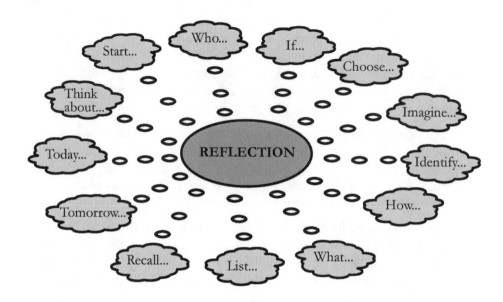

Figure 10-1: Thought starters for reflection.

If you need more than these words to begin the reflection process, use the following questions. You should use this first worksheet early in the service-learning process. You might revisit it as you progress through the experience.

Reflecting on the
Service-Learning Experience

Directions: Consider the following questions. Then write a well-thought-out response to each.

1. What am I feeling right now? Why am I feeling this way?

_____

_____

2. How do I interact with those around me?

_____

_____

3. How do those around me react when I am present?

_____

_____

4. What would I like to learn from this experience?

_____

_____

5. What are my top three to five priorities for this experience?

_____

_____

6. What are my goals?

_____

_____

Near the end of your service-learning experience, you may want to consider the following questions:

1. How has my initial impression changed?

2. How have my goals changed?

3. How did I grow?

4. How did I feel about my first visit, middle visit, and last visit?

Journal Writing

For some students, writing in a journal allows them to capture and reflect on their experiences effectively. Many students are able to communicate their thoughts best through paper and pen/pencil. Although journals are sometimes cumbersome, they can be written or read anywhere. The following worksheet shows the type of information you should capture in your journal.

Depending on the capabilities of your school, you could set up this reflection form on a Web site. You could also simply copy it into a hard-copy layout, perhaps as part of a reflection workbook. The layout should allow enough space for the responses and include separate pages for each day of the service-learning field work.

Reflection Worksheet

Date:_____ Course/Section: _____

Name:_____ Instructor: _____

Organization:_____ Location:_____

Date of visit:_____ Time: From_____To_____

Student reflection:
(Student reflects on his or her experience, taking into account a question or prompt from the instructor.)

_____

_____

_____

_____

_____

_____

Emotions checklist:

Excited ❏   Nervous ❏   Frustrated ❏   Satisfied ❏

What did I learn about myself today?

_____

_____

What did I learn about others today?

_____

_____

What did I learn about my course subject matter today?

_____

_____

How did my learning connect with my service?

_____

_____

What might be done to improve today's experience?

_____

_____

_____

_____

Discussion Boards

Many schools are networked with unique communication systems that facilitate communication among students and faculty. Creating reflections in an electronic format allows people to share and distribute their work more easily, especially when the entire class can benefit from the ideas shared by individuals. Electronic blackboards and discussion boards also allow instructors to provide feedback easily and in a timely manner.

The purpose of the discussion board is to allow students to reflect and respond to questions and/or experiences. There should be a balance between flexibility and structure. *Flexibility* means that if you experience something that wasn't anticipated, you have the opportunity to ask your instructor and classmates for input. *Structure* means that your instructor should ensure that the discussions relate to course content and provide a means for sharing experiences.

Checkout Assessments

Reflection opportunities may take place in the classroom, not just on the student's time. Using a "checkout assessment" is another opportunity for your instructor to see how you're doing. You complete the questions before you check out of that day's class.

Using a checkout assessment is a simple and quick way to assess the progress you're making. It also is a great way for you to provide feedback to the instructor without having to wait until the end of the semester. Checkout assessments can be used as frequently as your instructor wants. This tool provides another way to monitor your progress and allow for discussion.

Sample Checkout Assessment Form

Date: _____

Name: _____

Topic: _____

Something I have learned:

_____

_____

_____

I would have liked to have learned:

_____

_____

_____

My goal for my next time at the service-learning site is:

_____

_____

_____

Comments, suggestions, or concerns:

_____

_____

_____

Graphic Organizers

Logistically, taking notes using some form of graphic organizer may prove an easier way for you to record reflections. A *graphic organizer* is a document that has some organization to it. It allows you to capture information, observations, and thoughts in an efficient manner and is intended to help you organize your thoughts.

For instance, say you are at your site and are actively involved with people. Whipping out a notepad or PDA and beginning to take notes may not be realistic, or even polite. What does make sense, however, is to fill out a graphic organizer right after your experience. The following chart is designed to give you a general idea of areas to consider. Feel free to customize it and create your own organizer.

Sample Graphic Organizer #1

Directions: Consider the following questions. Then write an honest response to each. You can modify these questions each time you do a new reflection.

Environment: What is the place like? Is it what you expected?	**Location:** Where is the agency located? How do you feel traveling to the agency?
Tools: Do you need any special tools to do your job?	**Resources:** What resources does the agency use? Examples: social workers, teachers, scientists, governmental agencies.
Activities: What activities are you involved in? Describe the tasks, feelings, and skills you are learning.	**People:** Describe the people you are working with. What are their credentials, skills, personalities? Has someone helped you as a mentor?

Another type of graphic organizer can be used to capture information about the setting you're working in. Note that it provides you the opportunity to draw. Making a drawing of the layout will be helpful in the future as you look back on the experience and recall those physical features that made the site what it was.

This type of graphic organizer is especially helpful if you are working in a classroom. Every teacher sets up his or her classroom differently. This organizer provides a terrific opportunity to see different settings, make notes on them, and use the information to create your own ideal classroom. Perhaps in your future career, you'll be able to use this information to set up your own room.

Sample Graphic Organizer #2

Agency name:_____

Location:_____

Describe the place where your service-learning experience is taking place.

_____

_____

_____

Draw the place where your service-learning experience is taking place, including both the inside, outside, and so on.

(continued)

(continued)

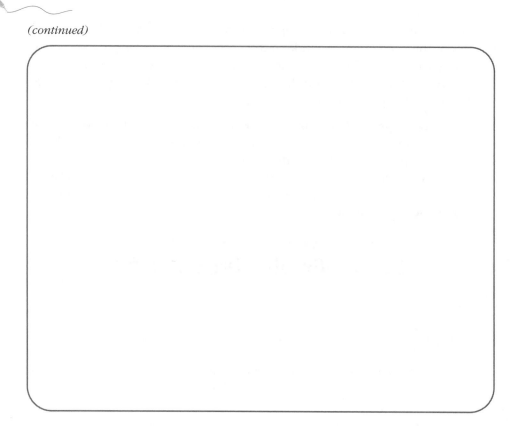

From Here...

As you can see, reflection is a personal process. How each person approaches and creates his or her reflections may be unique. Whichever styles you choose, remember to stretch your thoughts and ideas. Think outside the box. Meditate on those things that occurred, the reasons they occurred, and their outcomes. Be sure to coordinate a feedback process with your instructor. Learn to listen and grow from his or her comments. Most importantly, know that your reflections are truly indications of your energy, efforts, and enhanced knowledge about yourself and your service-learning setting.

In the next chapter, we help you to think about the final phase of your service-learning experience—saying a "good good-bye." As our students tell us: "It seems like we just got started, and now it is time to end our time...!"

CHAPTER 11

Ending the Service-Learning Experience

"This experience has so enveloped my being and shall forever be in my mind as well as my heart. In a heart that was once empty, has now become a sanctuary; full of experience, love and hope."

Maureen

Sometimes the ending phase of service-learning is poorly conceived and weakly developed because of the lack of planning. To keep your service-learning experience in your mind and heart, you need to have a "good good-bye." Such a good-bye includes a thoughtful plan to end the service-learning experience. Special attention to the acknowledgment of the relationships built during the service-learning partnership is vital for closure.

This chapter guides you in the development of activities to end your service-learning experience and describes the steps for assessing your personal growth, skill development, and achievement of course objectives. Although this is the final period of your service-learning experience, continued use of discussion and reflection activities is of utmost importance. In this chapter, you'll answer the following questions:

- How do I say good-bye in a celebratory way?

- How do I feel about saying good-bye? Have I made a difference?

- What is my plan to finalize service-learning activities and course requirements?

Planning for the end of a service-learning experience involves three areas of preparation to say good-bye: assessment, relationships, and activities. After the service-learning experience ends, you can take what you've learned on your service-learning journey to help you on your career path. This chapter suggests ways to connect your service-learning experience with your future career plans and provides examples of how to integrate the skills that you have developed and the service that you have provided into resumes and cover letters for future job applications.

Assessing Your Accomplishments

"I think learning for the sake of it is a wonderful thing, but I also think that if you have learned something, gained some knowledge, insight or whatever, then you have an obligation. I'm not exactly sure what it is, but I don't think that you can be the same person doing the same things, thinking the same way."

—Kezia

You cannot assess a service-learning experience through paper-and-pencil tests. This section provides several different assessment activities so that you can assess yourself based on your style of learning and the teacher's requirements. Get ready to stretch and express yourself in a variety of ways!

Parts of this section will require you to retrieve the list of objectives you created earlier. Use the following worksheet to list the objectives you had and accomplishments you achieved. Taking time to reflect on them is very important. We hope you will be pleasantly surprised and realize the progress you've made.

My Objectives and Accomplishments: Realistic or Ridiculous?

Directions: Refer back to "My Personal Learning Goals Map" worksheet from Chapter 3. Examine the objectives you had hoped to achieve. Pick the three objectives that are most important to you now. In the Accomplishments section, jot down the knowledge, skills, and attitudes that have changed, increased, or decreased as you reflect on your service-learning experience.

Important Objectives

1. _____

_____

2. _____

_____

3. _____

_____

Accomplishments

_____

_____

_____

_____

_____

_____

_____

Directions: Now take some time to reflect on the results. Read each of the following questions. Then provide an honest answer for each.

1. Were these objectives realistic?

_____

2. Were these objectives challenging, too challenging, or not challenging enough?

_____

(continued)

(continued)

3. Looking back, what objectives would you have changed?

_____

_____

_____

4. What did you learn that you were not expecting to learn?

_____

_____

_____

Teachers often use the following worksheet to assess their students' knowledge. We think it can be a useful tool when you're assessing how much you've learned in your service-learning course. If you and/or your teacher like the layout of it, then give it a try.

Don't rush into this worksheet, however. Take some time to truly reflect on your whole experience. See what kinds of responses you can come up with as you think back over the duration of your service-learning experience. Now is the time to pinpoint what you have learned to demonstrate—your knowledge, skills, and attitudes as a community-minded, caring person—with a college admissions officer, a prospective employer, or even another teacher.

At the same time, you are not expected to have the answers for community problems as a result of your service-learning experience. Students who are able to formulate a well-thought-out question based on what they saw, heard, or participated in often demonstrate much more insightfulness and intelligence than students who propose to have all the answers. So, to prepare your good-bye to the agency staff, the service-learning program participants, and your class instructor, write down your most significant thoughts related to what you learned, what you'd like to share, and questions you might still have.

Service-Learning Hindsight: Connecting Lessons Learned with My Next Steps

Directions: Take some time to reflect on your service-learning experience—from start to finish. Write honest, thoughtful, and detailed responses for each of the following items.

1. Things I learned:

   a._____

   b._____

   c._____

2. Things I wish to share:

   a._____

   b._____

   c._____

3. Questions I still have:

   a._____

   b._____

   c._____

Reflecting on Relationships and Saying Good-Bye

"I started to feel more comfortable with myself and with my abilities the day that one of the students came up to me and hugged me and thanked me for being there."

—Alisha

Throughout your service-learning experience, you had the opportunity to meet a variety of people. At the site, you likely met a supervisor, your leaders in the organization; the staff, who make things happen; and of course, the agency participants, who are often the recipients of your service. Saying good-bye to the people you learned to appreciate and who may have learned to count on you is *the* most important step to ensure a "good good-bye"!

Service-learning relationships can be extremely rewarding. The people you meet and your relationships with them are something you'll never forget. As part of the end of the experience, you should reflect on those people who made a difference in your learning experience. Using the following worksheet, take a moment to reflect on your service-learning relationships.

Reflecting on Who Taught Me and What I Learned

Directions: Consider the following questions. Then write your thoughtful response to each.

Staff/Program Recipients

1. Who did you interact with the most?

   _____

   _____

2. Name three things you learned from

   Staff at the agency:

   _____

   _____

   _____

Program recipients:

_____

_____

_____

3. How did your relationship with the staff and/or program help you to enhance your understanding of others? (Review Chapter 5 on cultural sensitivity.)

_____

_____

4. How did your relationship with the staff and/or program help you to enhance your understanding of yourself? (Review Chapter 5 on cultural sensitivity.)

_____

_____

5. What specific skills have you increased? (Review Chapters 6, 7, and 8 on skill development.)

   Did you grow in your ability to interact with people at the service-learning site? What skills did you use to interact with people? How? What happened?

_____

_____

   What do you think you might have taught people at the service-learning site? (Remember that learning is usually a two-way street.)

_____

_____

(continued)

(continued)

Service-Learning Site

1. How did you feel working at this site? (Think about the environment, people, and cultures.)

   _____

   _____

2. Do you feel more comfortable now than you did when you began your service-learning experience?

   _____

   _____

   Why?

   _____

   _____

   What has changed?

   _____

   _____

3. Do you think you made a difference?

   _____

   _____

   How and in what ways?

   _____

   _____

4. List some things you were able to accomplish and why they were important to you.

   _____

   _____

5. List some things you were unable to accomplish and why they were important to you.

_____

_____

6. What could have been done differently at the service-learning site to help you accomplish these goals?

_____

_____

Students with Their Teachers/Instructors

1. Did you find class discussions helpful?

_____

_____

2. Were you able to share problems you were having?

_____

_____

If not, why not? And what solutions would you suggest for the next time?

_____

_____

3. What would you still like to learn?

_____

_____

(continued)

(continued)

> 4. Do you feel "called" to any sort of activism or civic engagement?
>
> _____
>
> _____

Now that you've had a chance to reflect on the relationships you've developed, it is important to plan the steps you will take to say your final good-bye. Using the suggestions that follow will help make the end of your service-learning experience a pleasant one. It will help set the stage for your next educational or career move. You'll be asked to begin thinking of yourself as a professional, not just a student.

Going through the process as a class and role-playing the process of saying good-bye might be an excellent experience. The more opportunities you have to practice your "good good-byes," the more comfortable you'll be with the whole process. We offer one set of suggestions to say goodbye to the agency staff and a different set of suggestions for your good-bye to service-learning program recipients/participants.

Saying Good-Bye to the Agency Service-Learning Coordinator

Review your calendar and, based on your last service-learning visit, note an appropriate date that you want to officially say good-bye. Planning for this event shows that you are organized and prepared to end your experience on a positive note. Schedule this meeting, known as an *exit interview*, at least two weeks prior to the end of your session. Be sure to confirm the date and time with your service-learning coordinator.

The concept of an exit interview may sound a bit formal, but in reality it accomplishes several things. For example, it allows you to have some uninterrupted time with your service-learning coordinator.

Keep in mind that the exit interview is just as important as any other interview. Be sure to prepare with the same care because it's at this point that you move from being a student to being a professional. Follow these tips to make your last impression a good one.

- Review your goals and objectives and your journals to be clear about what you've accomplished. Be prepared to discuss your accomplishments with your service-learning coordinator.

- Attend to your personal hygiene. Be clean, and make sure your hair is neat and your breath is fresh.

- Dress appropriately. This is your opportunity to show the world that you are a professional. Wear the clothing necessary to gain respect in your chosen field.

- Shake hands with your service-learning coordinator at the beginning and end of the meeting. Your handshake should be firm, but not crushing. Stand up straight and tall, and look the person in the eyes when meeting. (Be sensitive to cultures that do not appreciate this type of hand or eye contact. Remember in Chapter 5 on cultural sensitivity we encouraged you to ask the people at the service-learning site about appropriate interpersonal actions.)

Although the exit interview has the potential to be an emotional time for both you and your service-learning coordinator, always remain professional. You might cover the following during the interview:

- Discuss the lessons you've learned. Review your goals and objectives.

- Allow your service-learning coordinator the opportunity to provide feedback and to say good-bye.

- Assuming the experience has been a successful one, you might ask your service-learning coordinator for a recommendation or reference letter. You also might ask whether he or she minds if you list him or her as a reference on a job application. However, if you don't think you'll receive a favorable recommendation, you might ask your coordinator if you have any reason to be concerned. In either case, you should never list someone as a reference without first obtaining his or her approval. First, it's a courtesy, and second, you want to make sure that person will portray you in a positive manner.

- Thank your service-learning coordinator.

After your experience has ended, remember to send your service-learning coordinator a thank-you letter.

Saying Good-Bye to Service-Learning Program Participants

Joy, Shawn, Yolanda, and Megan shared with us that their greatest learning came from their interaction and relationships with the service-learning program participants. Whether the program participants were youth members of a community center, elderly residents of a nursing home, community activists involved in neighborhood change, or inmates at the county jail, the students expressed that their biggest challenge was to say a "good good-bye" to these service-learning partners.

"What do I do? What do I say? I feel sad. Can't I just leave—I'll visit again…" are often statements that students make a month prior to the end of their service-learning project. The following suggestions will help you prepare.

Step #1: Begin Saying Good-Bye on the First Day

You begin to say good-bye on the first day of your service-learning experience. Inform your service-learning partners of the duration of your time with them. A calendar or a big poster with the actual dates/times and ending dates you will be on-site is a useful, visible reminder of the actual length of time you will be at the service-learning site. However, that visible reminder is typically not sufficient. It is important for you to casually remind everyone each week of your last service-learning date at the site. Saying something like "Remember, we have X number of remaining visits together" each week helps to lessen the sense of surprise at the end. Do *not* wait until the last week and say, "Oh, by the way, this is my last week."

Step #2: End the Experience without Feel-Good, Make-Believe Promises

When you finally say good-bye, be realistic and say it. Don't pretend that you will be back to visit after the service-learning has ended. Everyone understands that your time was limited and you would eventually go on to other things. Don't give the false impression that you're going to be back to visit or stay in touch. When you make good-intentioned promises but are not able to keep them, you create distrust and hurtful feelings in the people you learned to care about. Those hurt feelings may also carry over to the next group of service-learning students. Saying good-bye is never easy, but it is necessary. Get on with the next phase in your life, and enjoy it.

If you have been offered employment at the agency or the service-learning site, congratulations! But you *still* need to end the service-learning relationship and move on to your relationship with the people at the service-learning site as a member of the staff. As a student who is completing service-learning, you have one set of expectations and responsibilities. However, if at any time during your experience you become an employee, you need to help others—including your instructor—to understand that your role has changed.

Step #3: Determine a Safe Place to Send Future Correspondence or Make Contact

We encourage you not to give out your home address, e-mail address, or phone number to service-learning participants. This creates a false sense of future contact. If you feel inclined to correspond with service-learning participants, get permission to send your correspondence to the agency.

Planning Good-Bye Activities

Now for the fun part! Ending a service-learning experience on a positive note involves interactive, reflective, and happy activities. Ending activities give the participants (including the students, staff, and teacher) a chance to celebrate the end of a successful journey. There are various ways you can plan an ending celebration. The option you choose will depend on people's ages, abilities, schedules, location, and, of course, the cost of celebrating. We encourage you to discuss your ideas with your service-learning coordinator. Although surprises are fun, you need to develop your ending activities with approval, input, and, if possible, a budget allocation from the service-learning coordinator.

Use the following list to determine the issues you'll need to plan around and activities you should consider:

- **Time:** Poll the people you wish to invite to determine their availability.

- **Cost:** Determine how much everything will cost and the process to requisition or be reimbursed for supplies.

- **Transportation:** If you plan an outing, figure out how people will get there.

- **Safety/Permission/Insurance:** Don't forget to plan for all these issues, especially if you're working with young people.

- **Gifts:** Consider giving a gift to the people you've worked with at the service-learning site. The gift needs to be a simple expression of your appreciation. Some students create appreciation certificates to express a unique quality of each person with whom they developed a special relationship. The gift doesn't have to be expensive; it's the thought that counts!

One service-learning group ended their experience by inviting the youths they were working with back to the college campus. The service-learning participants enjoyed seeing where the college students lived and what college life was like. The campus visit was a real eye-opener for some of the youths, as well as the students. Through conversations, it was evident that this visit triggered an interest to go on to college. The young people looked up to the college students and saw the opportunity for them to go to school. The college students motivated the young people to consider the importance of going on to college and that doing so wasn't impossible. They discussed the practical side of getting into college, plus the importance of completing high school and doing well. It's hard to say, but this short visit may have had a direct impact on the future of these young people.

On the other hand, some of the college students realized for the first time that not everyone had the same level of emotional and financial support that they had. The youths from the community center introduced the college students to the reality of economic disparities in our country. Both groups learned a lasting lesson as a result of a fun, educational ending activity.

Another service-learning class ended their experience in a multicultural way. Food was the centerpiece of this event. All attendees were asked to bring a dish to pass that was native to their culture. The conversations started flowing when the food came out. Food seems to have a way of letting people relax and be themselves. Sharing dishes from your own culture is a neat way of letting those you've been working with find out a little more about you personally.

Connecting Service-Learning with Your Career Plans

Now that your service-learning experience is coming to a close, it's time to seriously consider how you can incorporate your experience and lessons learned into your next education or career move. It's never too soon to begin planning for your career. Begin creating your resume early. Don't wait until you graduate. You'll find that if you begin creating and building your resume early, finalizing it will be easier in the long run. Consider the reflections you completed earlier in this chapter. The information in those reflections may help you develop your resume or complete applications.

You can display information on a resume in various ways. Generally, you'll find that the information included on the resume is fairly consistent. It should include

- Name, address, city, state, ZIP, phone, e-mail

- Objective (optional)

- Background summary (optional)

- Experience

- Academic background, education, and/or professional credentials

- Professional organizations

Let's review some ways you can identify and create descriptions of your service-learning experience. Use the following worksheet to determine which methods are appropriate for you and to begin building your own resume.

Developing My Resume

Directions: Do the following tasks.

1. Brainstorm those activities and skills you used during your service-learning experience.

2. Review those activities and sort them into the following categories (some examples have been provided for you):

Specific Activities:	**Skills Learning:**
homework	reading a map
reading	software
interviews	teamwork
food-cupboard	

(continued)

(continued)

3. Write down at least five action verbs that relate to the activities or skills you've learned. Some suggestions are assessed, mentored, or organized.

_____   _____

_____   _____

_____   _____

_____   _____

4. For each of the words you listed, write short descriptions of what you did. Here are some examples:

Assisted children in grades 4–8 with their homework. These children were part of an urban after-school program.

Designed a program for collecting, sorting, and distributing food to the unemployed.

_____

_____

_____

_____

_____

The descriptions that you just created can be used not only on a resume but within a job application and cover letter as well. Employers are always impressed when individuals can articulate the skills and experiences they've had. Keep these descriptions in mind as you plan for potential job interviews. Also, be sure to follow up with a thank-you letter. You'll find that being able to tell others what your skills and experiences are and how those skills can benefit their company is valuable.

Sample Resume

Name
Street City, ST ZIP
Home Phone: (xxx) xxx-xxxx Cell Phone: (xxx) xxx-xxxx
E-mail Address

Education

College, Location, Degree, Major

High School, Location

Experience and Work History

Depending on the type of career you're seeking, you might list professional and field experiences separately.

You also have the choice of listing experiences sequentially by date or by the type of experience.

Be sure to include the date, location, and description of the experience. Use action verbs to describe your experience. Here is one example:

Fall 20XX: Participated in a service-learning course in which we interviewed residents at a county health facility. We then documented and created a scrapbook displaying their lives.

Skills/Assets or Accomplishments

- Communicate well with people
- Motivate and encourage people
- Have excellent work ethic
- Organize and coordinate events
- Use this software: Word, Excel, PowerPoint, Access, Project

Volunteer Activities

List any offices you've held and activities you've been involved in.

Professional Associations

List any associations in which you are a member, and note any offices you have held.

References

List the name, title, address, and phone number of people who have agreed to act as references for you. Be sure to include the teacher who taught the service-learning class and the service-learning coordinator.

Sample Cover Letter

Date

Name
Title
Company/Organization
Street
City, ST ZIP

Salutation: Use Ms. or Mr.; try to use the person's name.

Paragraph #1: State why you are writing; identify the position you are applying for.

Paragraph #2: Summarize your primary qualifications for the job in one sentence. Give a specific example showing how you've used these skills.

Paragraph #3: Discuss how service-learning has helped you to be prepared for the world of work. Give specific examples of the types of service you provided. Discuss how this activity and the skills you learned relate to the position you are applying for.

Paragraph #4: End the letter by asking for an interview or meeting.

Sincerely,

Signature
Name
Street
City, ST ZIP
Phone (day, evenings)
Cell phone
E-mail

From Here...

We can't emphasize enough the importance of your good-bye to bring positive closure to your experience—whether or not you achieved *all* your initial goals. In this chapter, you had the opportunity to plan for the successful completion of your service-learning project. In addition, you had the opportunity to assess your progress in relationship to the goals and objectives you set early in the program. You also had the chance to assess and reflect on the relationships that you developed along with way. We provided tools to help you prepare for the job application and interviewing process to incorporate your service-learning experience.

We hope that you have learned and have grown throughout this experience. In addition, we hope that you have developed the self-confidence necessary to move to the next step in your education or career.

One student who took a service-learning course stated, "[In a regular classroom]...we never get a chance to truly work with one another. By doing the service-learning as a group I learned so much about everyone's skills and techniques of interacting with and advocating for the students. It allowed me to see different skills expressed and I was able to learn new ways to approach a situation. I grew so much through this class."

As with this student, we hope that you will continue to see the connection between your service with others, your education, and the way you develop as a person and a professional. Good luck!

List of Resources

Albert, G. (1996). Intensive service-learning experiences. In Jacoby, Barbara (Ed.), *Service-learning in higher education* (p. 204). San Francisco: Jossey-Bass.

Fisher, Irene. S. (1996). Service-learning in higher education concepts and practices. In Jacoby, Barbara Editor (Ed), *Service-learning in higher education* (pp.208–228). San Francisco: Jossey-Bass.

Florida International University. 101 ideas for combining service & learning. www.fiu.edu/~time4chg/Library/ideas.html.

Gardner, Howard (1993). *Multiple intelligences, The theory in practice, A Reader*. New York: Basic Books.

Hobart and William Smith Colleges. Service learning. www.hws.edu/academics/enrichment/servicelearning.asp.

Indiana University-Purdue University at Indianapolis. IUPUI principles of student learning. www.imir.iupui.edu/IUPUIfolio/teach/teach_pul.htm.

Jacoby, B. (1996). *Service-learning in higher education*. San Francisco: Jossey-Bass.

Loeb, P. R. (1999). *Soul of a citizen*. New York: St. Martin's Griffen.

Michigan Journal of Community Service-Learning. (Volume 8, Fall 2001, pages 12 and 13). Ann Arbor, Michigan: OCSL Press, the publication arm of the Edward Ginsberg Center for Community Service and Learning, University of Michigan.

Mintz, S. and Hesser, G. (1996). Principles of good practice in service-learning. In Jacoby, Barbara (Ed.), *Service-learning in higher education* (p. 204). San Francisco: Jossey-Bass.

Morton, K. (1996). Issues related to integrating service-learning into the curriculum. In Jacoby, Barbara (Ed.), *Service-learning in higher education* (p. 287). San Francisco: Jossey-Bass.

Nazareth College Center for Service-Learning. www.naz.edu/dept/service-learning/.

University of Utah. U of U service-learning scholars give 4,800 hours of community service. www.utah.edu/unews/releases/03/may/service.html.

Webster's New World Dictionary (Second Concise Ed.) (1978). New York: Avenel.

Youth Voices. Links. www.human.cornell.edu/youthvoices/links.cfm.

Index

worksheets